One Teacher's Times, My Life of Rhymes

by Leona M. Smith

Edited by Lori L. Smith

A Leona M. Smith Original

TABLE OF CONTENTS

2. Scottish Highlands, Leesburg, Florida

5. The Waterford, Perrysburg, Ohio

Postscript

[This page intentionally left blank.]
[Okay, nearly blank.]

PREFACE

I wrote our family history for the Benton County, Indiana History Project. It appeared on pages 268 and 269 of the 1987 edition.

SMITH-HERAMB

Wayne Allen Smith (9-20-30)
Leona May Smith (10-15-30)
Lisa Elaine Smith (1-16-59)
Lori Lynn Smith (8-18-62)

Wayne and Leona Smith
With daughters two in tow,
Took jobs in Benton County
To watch their children grow.

This event took place in August
In the year of '63,
Though years have slipped away
They are still there you see.

Wayne is the stern, strict principal
Of the Oxford public school,
And Leona, a third grade teacher
Who expounds the Golden Rule.

Wayne was often asked
How they functioned side by side,
"I am the boss at school," he said,
"But, at home she rules with pride."

Wayne's roots go back to England
Where father Albert was born,
Whose toil in dusty coal mines
At twelve he learned to scorn.

Albert and two of his brothers,
When they became young men,
Set sail for mighty America
To begin their lives again.

Albert settled in Terre Haute

Where he claimed a winsome wife,
And he and Thirza E. Brammer
Lived out their married life.

Wayne Allen was the youngest
Of their family of five,
Two brothers and two sisters
Kept the household quite alive.

High school graduation came
In nineteen forty-eight.
Purdue followed in 'fifty-two
And then he met his fate.

Fate came in the form of a female.
Leona Heramb was her name.
She was a senior at ISU
And teaching was her game.

Leona came of a sturdy pair
Whose children numbered thirteen.
Mass production was a way of life
Built into the daily routine.

Their farm was a mini-factory
With all hands pitching in
To sew up clothes, or fill up jars,
Or clean out the potato bin!

The union of Leona's parents
Must have been blessed from up above,
To provide for a big mob of children
Yet nurture them all with love.

Wayne and Leona were married
In December of 'fifty-three.

While he served two years in the army,
She completed her Master's Degree.

Then Wayne re-entered Purdue,
His teaching license to get,
While Leona taught at Durgan
Where she learned a lot you can bet.

There followed four years at Rockville
With Wayne at the local school.
Leona taught classes at Hillsdale
'Til Lisa was born to rule.

An offer came from Linden,
They pulled up stakes right then.
Wayne became a principal
And Leona was pregnant again.

Lori arrived upon the scene
To make the family complete,
And Lisa had a sister
With whom she could compete.

That's when they moved to Oxford,
And you're back where you began
To read this sagging saga
Of one Benton County clan.

Both daughters went to Oxford School
Where they learned to read and write.
They found that being the principal's kids
Wouldn't help them in a fight.

The girls went on to B.C. High,
And time flew by so fast,
They learned a lot, they had some fun,
Then high school days were past.

Lisa majored in music
With degrees from ISU.

She followed in her parents' footsteps,
Now she's a teacher, too.

Lori earned her Bachelor's
In business from Ball State,
She thinks that getting a Master's
In Library Science would be great.

Our thanks to you dear reader
For sticking with this tale;
It's hoped the rhymes amused you
'Cause the story's rather pale.

Let it be said when the Smiths are dead
They devoted their lives to learning.
Monetary gains were nice to have
But satisfaction is what they were
earning.

Clockwise from left: Lori Smith, Timothy Brakel,
Lisa (Smith) Brakel, Wayne Smith, Leona Smith.

CHAPTER 1
OXFORD, INDIANA

THE DEED HAS BEEN DONE
1980

Poems, perhaps, have a reason,
Mine was the flimsiest one.
No store close at hand sold greetings,
No time to make a long run.

Thus began My Life of Rhyme
Which was bred to fill a need;
Some deemed my efforts amusing.
Others endured my dire deed.

Be that as it may, my dear readers,
I've enjoyed my poetic fun,
With the binding of this collection,
I'll consider My Life of Rhyme
Is closed.
It's now done.

This poem accompanied a gift of a birdhouse and some jelly for second grade teacher, Thelma Moyars. I think I wrote it in 1970.

THE BIRDHOUSE

At this, another Christmastide,
We pause a moment to remember
The times long gone in ages past
And the trails we used to wander.

Consider lost, the 'backyard path—
In cold and freezing weather,
The long line, waiting there
When families got together.

Consider the bubbly sticky goo
Of jelly in the making,
The first sweet taste licked from the spoon
And biscuits in the oven baking.

The next three poems were written on March 20, 1972 for three of my brothers.

For my brother, Herbert Eugene Heramb, on his birthday.

PORTNOY'S COMPLAINT

No use to worry,
No need to fret,
For it happens to most
When older they get.

So don't despair
For what just ain't,
You think *you've* got troubles?
Read *Portnoy's Complaint!*

For my brother, Virgil Ross Heramb (Red), on his birthday, March 20, 1972. He and Herb shared the same birth date but Red was 5 years older than Herb. This was for Red. We gave him an over-sized coffee cup.

WHEN ALL YOUR FUNNIN'S BEEN FUNNED OUT

When all your funnin's
Been funned out,
And all your uppins'
Is down and out,

And you're just feelin'
The need of a spree
Remember you're older
And it just may be

That all you need
Is a GREAT BIG CUP
Of good old coffee
To pick you up!

For my brother, Leon Ray Heramb. We gave him two dollars.

HAPPY ANNIVERSARY LEON AND BETTY

To celebrate your anniversary right
Take Betty out to dine one night,
And just to prove that we're not tight,
We'll pay the *tip*,
Now ain't that bright?

****

In October of the 1979-80 schoolyear, I wrote the following narrative poem to accompany a slide presentation for the local Board depicting just one day of daily activities at Oxford Elementary School in Oxford, Indiana where my husband, Wayne A. Smith, was the principal and I taught third grade.

A DAY AT OXFORD SCHOOL
1980

The start of each day
In the life of our school
Begins with this axiom
This one golden rule.

The doors must be opened;
We mean opened W-I-D-E
To allow all of the children
To hurry inside.

Each day is an adventure
As we open new doors
For our brains will be taxed
With new ideas we explore.

The opening of doors
Is like opening minds,
We search every facet
To see what we'll find.

Mr. Smith greets the teachers
With messages galore,
But on checking their boxes
They only find more.

He also greets children
Who don't ride a bus,
He's a pretty good doorman
For an ornery old cuss!

This child is ready
To greet the new day
WIth shoes on the wrong feet
He can walk, but which way?

Pretty soon all the buses
Start to arrive.
Things really start humming
As the school comes alive.

Students scurry to classrooms
Dispersing their things
And are ready to start
When the second bell rings.

With the Pledge to the Flag
We commence each school day,
We're proud of this country
And the American way.

The chosen ones scatter
Statistics to deliver;
They go straight to the office
With nary a quiver.

The lunch bags pile up
For Mary Louise Copas
But she never shrugs
And says that it's hopeless!

She doesn't just gossip
When the telephone rings,
But receives many calls
About sick kids and things.

Mr. Smith's at his desk now
In his office that glistens,
When a problem arises
Rest assured that he listens.

The thing that's protruding
From the front of his head
Is a pacifier for smoking--
He took up toothpicks instead.

Writer of the Month
Is really a big deal
Mr. Smith treats the winners
To a McDonald's meal.

5

He also gives preference
To Citizens of the Month;
They get Pepsi at recess
And potato chips to munch.

Miss Mary Jo Windler
Always starts class on time.
She thinks teaching kindergarten
Is really sublime.

The Learning Center teacher
Is smiling Mrs. Larch,
She writes many prescriptions,
Student minds she will spark.

Now, who is that trailing
Her in this picture?
He should march in a line
But, by golly, he's tricked her!

One of her students
Wants so much to ride,
So extra time is allowed him
In the parking lot outside.

Her aide, Mrs. Sturgeon,
Was replaced by Jo Bice,
And although we miss Shirley
We've found Bice is nice.

The TMR class
Is a challenge, that's true,
But if you can't pronounce Dickman
You can surely say Sue.

There are lots of special lessons
Such as riding this bike
They do a great many things
So school work they'll like.

Mrs. Marcelline Ruwe,
Our Teacher of the Year,
Has to speak loudly
So all of us can hear.

We must stay on the lines
When we're printing our name
And complete all of our work
Or we can't play a game.

In Mrs. Richard's room
Our second grade learned
How to make bread
And it didn't even burn!

Our room must be pretty
So she showed us the way
To make clever turkeys
To create a display.

Our teacher, Mrs. Feuer
Also helped us make bread,
And, would you believe it?
It turned out like she said!

But look at this problem
That's written on the board
You can just bet your boots,
It won't be ignored.

If your...forehead's on fire
And your...tum-a-lum...hurts
You can...stagger...down the hallway...
And consult with the nurse.

Usually, Nurse Geswein
Is a very kind person,
But when you see THAT GREAT BIG
NEEDLE
You're hurtin' for certain!

If she is not there,
Mrs. Copas will help.
She's always so gentle,
There's never a whelp.

Those measles shots were horrid.
We didn't like them one bit!
But, guess it was better

Than having those zits!

Every Wednesday morning,
When the second bell rings,
In comes Nurse Geswein
And we all do our thing.

You must rinse just one minute—
No less and no more.
Then spit it back in the cup
But not on the floor.
(Fluoride treatments which are now
added to our water supply.)

It's now time for recess.
The children go outside;
Some rush to the swings
And others to the slide.

Some will play kickball
And others will climb,
But, finding an Indian bead
Is really sublime.

The fifth and the sixth graders
Race 'cross the yard
For a fast game of basketball
On a surface that's hard.

For third grade and fourth grade,
The saddle's the thing,
But most will play kickball
Till the recess bell rings.

It's back to the books, now,
For recess is through
We'll visit more classes
And see what they do.

Our Mrs. Sina Smith
Teaches third grade, you know,
With all her fine teaching
We'll grow and we'll grow.

Here is Mr. Duncan
Who auctioned off books;
You can tell we were eager
From the way that it looks.

In our third grade class,
Mrs. Smith is our teacher,
But when it comes to reading
She's more like a preacher!

She's a stickler for details
Such as capitals and periods
She points out our errors;
Sure does make one weary.

Miss Tilton in fourth grade
Keeps us busy, that's true.
But we really don't mind it,
'Cause she's so pretty, too.

We must write every problem.
The whole bloomin' thing!
Or we know she will scold
Till our ears start to ring.

Carolyn Krebs and Judy Hedrick,
Our fine teachers' aides,
Always work hard
For they help all of the grades.
They conduct special reading
Where they polish some skills
With the basic component
Being drill, drill, drill.

Mrs. Wilkins teaches students
The library to use,
They learn to respect books
And never to abuse.

Each class in the school
Makes use of the library;
They'll learn to use it well
If they are not too contrary.

Yes the library's a classroom.
It is, sure enough.
But it can also be a refuge
When the going gets tough.

When this picture was taken
She had put in her bid
To be a bouncy cheerleader
But she lost—so she "hid."

These library helpers
Wear special attire
Designed by Mrs. Wilkins
To inflate egos higher.

It's time to have lunch now,
To the lunch room we go.
That's part of our school work
For bodies, too, must grow.

Our two smiling cooks,
Mrs. Swim and Pat Scott
Serve up luscious portions
Of food that is hot.

There's little doubt about it
When Krebs and Hedrick in charge.
There can be no horsing around
In a lunchroom this large.

Lunch now is over.
It's recess again
So it's back to the ballgame,
I wonder who'll win.

A stray dog or cat
May roam down the hall
But if it's a BIRD
(Bill Bird, curriculum coordinator)
The whole school stands tall!

Or a parent may come
To talk to a teacher
We try to point out

Each good and bad feature.

We attempt to leave them smiling
Hoping they'll share our load
For educating children
Can be a very rocky road.

Personal calls may be made
From the booth down the hall
But we mustn't write graffiti
All over the wall.

Noon recess must end
As most good times do,
They never last long enough
That one sure flew!

We take turns on restrooms
And line up for drinks,
It's a necessary part
Of our school day we think.

Mrs. Wade likes our fifth grade;
We've already begun
To master those facts.
Sometimes learning is fun.

She's a very fine person
And is always precise,
She expects lots from us,
But she's still pretty nice.

Mr. John Johnson
Likes our fifth grade, too
We often do experiments
To prove something is true.

This time we're lucky,
And it turned out okay
With science class over,
We've had a good day.

Our teacher's Mrs. Lambert,
She's new here this year.

Anytime we need help,
We know that she's near.

She's not a bit stupid
But quite bright, you know,
So on every project
Our brilliance must show.

Mr. Benedict is our teacher.
He surely does look tough.
We mind our own business
'Cause he can get rough!

When we can't find an answer,
We know we must ask
For those sixth grade subjects
Are really a task.

Here is our mail woman
Does that boggle your mind
Perhaps you're like me,
Just wondering...what kind?

Well, it's finally last recess
But look! Yuk! It's raining!
We'll have to play inside.
There's no use complaining.

So pull out the games, pals,
We'll play in our rooms;
We don't get the gym
And it looks like we're doomed.

A few lucky teachers
Get to go to the lounge
For some change of pace chatter
Or some coffee to scrounge.

Now, should we have coffee
With the price out of sight?
Or pop at 35 cents?
Well, neither price is right.

Last recess is over

So let's continue our tour
Of the more special classes,
You'll like them, I'm sure.

We stretch and bend
When we go to Phys. Ed
For Mr. Rogers, our teacher,
We use both bodies and heads.

We do calisthenics
Or work on some skills,
Or, perhaps play a game
Punctuated with thrills.

In music, the teacher
Is talented Mrs. Trost;
When it comes to good music,
She is the most.

When the fifth and the sixth graders
Got their new horns,
Under her direction,
Musicians were born.

Mrs. Brenda McDowell,
Art teacher supreme,
Never has time
To just sit and dream.

As one of her duties,
She picks Artist of the Week,
Puts their work in the library,
And we all sneak a peek.

M-m-McLaren, M-M-M-McFerren
N n now, uh-uh, wh-wh-wh-what is her
n-n-name?
W-w-well, w-w-whatever it is
Sp-sp-eech is her game.

During this part of the day
We have holiday celebrations.
We'll show just a few
Of our Halloween creations.

The big Raggedy Ann
Is our kindergarten teacher
If you just look around
You'll see many a creature.

And here's Mrs. Ruwe
In her holiday togs,
The only thing missing
Was trained golliwogs!

The second grade clown
Was a big one, you see—
Some mothers like parties,
Don't you agree?

I see a parent here
And also another,
Who likes parties best?
The child or his mother?

The fifth grade had everything,
Even Siamese twins!
Woodstock found the fourth grade
And sneaked right on in.

Inimitable Deb Davis,
As the witch, Baba Yaga,
Thrilled all the kids
With her Halloween Saga.

The sixth grade decided
To commemorate this day,
So they asked Mrs. Larch
To direct them in a play.

She gladly responded
And they gave it their best.
The whole school enjoyed it,
It was a delightful success.

They presented her a plaque
So she would remember that day.
She surely won't forget
Either them or the play.

The clock on the wall
Shows it is now 3:17.
The students all exit
And go home to their dreams.

The buses load up
And pull away from the curb.
They'll be delivered home safely
You can all rest assured.

The teachers will leave now
Though their work is not done
They'll take some of it home
For an evening of fun.

The building is quiet,
There is hardly a sound.
The classrooms are empty
And no one around.

But, wait, there's a noise!
Now, what can that be?
The custodians are cleaning,
Sure they are, don't you see?

They're disposing of papers
And wiping things clean.
They'll sweep the floors
With that giant machine.

They'll work while the Brownies
Have an after school session
And all through the ballgame
In steady progression.

They'll hear all the cheering
That comes from the gym
As the crowd yell for Oxford,
Hoping their team will win.

No matter which sex
Is playing the game,
The noise from the gym
Will sound much the same.

When the ballgame is over
And they've called the last play,
They'll turn out the lights,
And call it a day.

As they lock up the building,
The security's set.
Well, we're ready for tomorrow
Which might…turn… out… to…be
OUR….BEST….DAY….YET!

****

At one point in time I thought I would like to try writing children's stories. The following is one attempt.

BIGELOW, BIGELOW, BIGELOW BEAR
1980

Papa Bear and Bigelow Bear
Went out to take a walk.
Said Papa Bear to Bigelow Bear,
"We need to have a talk."

"You have not been a good bear,
You will make your mother wild
If you don't do your very best
To be a good bear child."

Said Bigelow Bear to Papa Bear,
"But Papa I do try.
How could I know the pet I got
Would make my Mama cry?"

"I did not want the frog I had
To hop into the stew,
I put him down, and said to him,
'Now do be good, please do.'"

"I did my best, I really did,
So why are you so mad?
I did say please like Mama said
I think you should be glad."

Said Papa Bear to Bigelow,
"You know I'm proud of you,
But you must never let a frog
Hop into Mama's stew."

"You can go and play now,
But do try to be good.
You must be nice to Mama
Act the way you should."

Bigelow saw a big, brown rock
Lying on the ground,
It was the very best one
That he had ever found.

He took it to his Mama
So she could really see
Just how good a bear child
Her little bear could be.

"Mama, Mama, may I
Put this rock here by the door?
It will keep the door wide open
And will help to dry the floor."

Said Mama Bear to Bigelow,
"Yes, put it by the door,
I have to do some shopping,
So I must hurry with this floor."

Bigelow did as Mama said
And he was very proud
For hadn't he said, "May I?"
He had said it very loud.

11

"Bigelow, Bigelow, Bigelow Bear?"
He heard his Mama yell.
"You get that turtle out of here!
Or Papa I will tell!"

Bigelow's eyes popped open.
Now, what had happened here?
How could there be a turtle
Scaring Mama dear?

He ran right in and saw it
Crawling all around.
It was not a rock at all
But a turtle he had found.

Papa Bear and Bigelow Bear
Went out to take a walk.
Said Papa Bear to Bigelow,
"We have to have a talk."

"You have not been a good bear,
You have made your Mama sad,
And if you don't do better,
I am going to get mad!"

Said Bigelow to Papa Bear,
"But, Papa, don't you see?
I was only showing Mama
What a good bear I could be."

"I did my best, I really did.
So why are you so mad?
I even asked her, 'may I?'
I think you should be glad."

Said Papa Bear to Bigelow,
"You know I'm glad, my son
But you must leave your pets outside
When you are having fun."

Bigelow went on his way
But walking, oh so sloo-o-ow
When he saw a big, big pretty place
Where lots of roses grow.

He picked some for his Mama
So she would not be so mad.
When she saw the pretty roses
She wouldn't think he was so bad.

Bigelow put the roses
Where his Mama, dear, could see,
How could he know that the hum he heard
Was the buzzing of a BEE!?

When Mama Bear came into the room,
She sat down on a chair,
The bee flew out an LANDED!!!!
Smack dab in her HAIR!!

Bigelow saw the buzzing bee
And tried to make it leave,
But then the bee flew after him
And landed on his sleeve.

"BIGELOW! BIGELOW! BIGELOW
BEAR!!!!"
He heard his Mama shout!
"GO JUMP INTO THE POOL," she said.
So Bigelow ran right out.

He fell into the water
And hugged a rock to hide.
If he had not been so wet,
He surely would have cried.

"Bigelow, Bigelow, Bear! "
He heard his mama say.
"Come on out of the water now,
The bee has gone away."

Bigelow was dripping wet.
He was a sight to see,
How could he know that this big mess
Would be caused by just one bee?

"I did my best, I really did,"
Cried Bigelow feeling sad.

"The roses meant I LOVE YOU, Mom.
So please don't think I'm bad."

Bigelow learned a lesson then,
He would not soon forget,
Mamas love you most it seems,

When you are soaking wet.

His Mama held him in her arm
She hugged him tight like this.
And got a BIG BEAR KISS?

****

WEDDING SHOWER FOR MARGARET HENSLEY
August 1982

Dear bride-to-be Margaret,
Of this paper and card please take note
I sent my husband to buy it;
His selection just didn't get my vote.

He knew it was meant for a SHOWER
Not a wedding as inscribed in the verse,
But the card MIGHT have said HAPPY
BIRTHDAY
So I guess that he could have done worse.

Impulsively, I thought I would pitch it
And run to the store to buy more
But the teacher inside wouldn't let me
So at the risk of being a bore---

Your lesson today, my dear Margaret
Is simply, concisely this;
When YOU send YOUR husband shopping
Give him a w-e-l-l d-e-f-i-n-e-d
CAPITALIZED LIST!!!

FOR MARILYNN BIRD'S 50TH BIRTHDAY
Aug. 21, 1983

Birthdays come,
Birthdays go,
Few compare
With the big "5 – oh."

Traumatic, perhaps,
But, then, maybe not,

Ponder the HALF CENTURY (!)
Of WISDOM you've got!

Flaunt all that wisdom!
Start a business that's a howler!
Palm yourself off
As "The Guru of Fowler!"

FOR THE OXFORD SCHOOL STUDENT BODY
Feb. 18, 1983

On President's Day
Mr. Smith will be gone,
But we'll be in school
We'll still carry on.

The man in the office
Will be different that day;
He's a man you *should* know
And he'll be looking your way.

13

The suit he'll be wearing
Has a very different style;
When he walks down the hall,
Give him a wave and a smile.

What man do you know
Who wears red, white, and blue?

What man stands for our country,
The brave and the true?

You'll meet him on Monday
You'd better be good
And be patriotic
And act like you should!

****

For the Ken and Betty Harris family after their house, which was next door to ours, burned sometime in the spring of l982 or 1983, I think. I enclosed a double four leaf clover with the poem.

FIRE-PROOF
1983

We hope this will help you
To buy what you need,
But there's one word of caution
We feel you should heed.

If the item isn't marked
In great...big...**bold...letters,**
FIRE-PROOF AND **THEFT-PROOF**
DON'T buy it! You can do better.

****

The only poem for which I was ever paid appeared in the March 1982 issue of THE FARM JOURNAL magazine. My daughter, Lori, wrote the last line of the poem so we were listed as co-authors. We received $100 for the poem. I originally wrote the poem for a roast at a staff dinner to honor Marcia Chinn. She and her husband had just moved to a farm.

HOW TO CALL HOGS
!1982

Now iffen you folks
Has moved back to the farm,
And you're hankerin' to soak up
That good country charm,
They's jest a few things that
Ya oughta be knowin'
Least iffen it's hogs
You's plannin' on growin'.

Now piggies is fine

When they's jest little fellers,
They's as cute as a punkin
And as tame as Old Yeller,
But when they's growed bigger
And is sportin' a snout,
That's when all you ladies
Had better watch out.

They's mean ornery critters,
They'll bust outa the pen!

Iffen yer hubby ain't home,
They'll do it right then.
You'll be chasin', and soueyin',
And runnin' through the weeds,
An' this ain't the kinda life
That any lady needs.

So all ya gotta learn
Is how to call hogs
An' that can be easier
Than fallin' off a log.
Jest hook up a CB
Twixt hubby and you,
Then when the pigs gets out,

This is all ya do.
Get hubby on the CB
And say, oh, so sweet,
"Iffen ya comes home quick hon,
I'll give ya a treat."
If you's said it jest right,
He should come a runnin'
But when he sees them pigs,
He'll know you wuz funnin'.

Jest advice fer callin' hogs
Is all you'll find here,
An' how you'll handle hubby?
That's YORE problem, dear

The editor of THE FARM JOURNAL encouraged me to send in more poems to them in the future—and, he said, that they didn't normally print poems. I did send in one other poem to him. He said it was so short that it wouldn't fill up enough space but, he added, if I could write another one to go with it, they might publish them. Unfortunately, I was a teacher. There was little time in my schedule for any "fun stuff" like writing poems. This is the second poem I submitted to them.

A TACTLESS MAN

I once served some gravy for dinner
Which obviously should have been thinner.
"It's interesting," daughter said
Looking at it with dread.
She, too, knew it wasn't a winner.

My husband surreptitiously did eye it
'Til he finally found nerve enough to try it.
"It's substantial," he observed
Since his fork it had curved,
"Perhaps Ace Construction might buy it!"

****

The following poems were written to accompany gag gifts for a few of the people attending Oxford School's Spring Teacher's Dinner, May 21, 1982.

For Sina Smith, a small wooden rocking chair. She had just become a grandmother.

Modern grandmas flit
With nary a care
But old-fashioned ones sit
In a good rocking chair.

For Mary Louise Copas who had just suffered a fall on the ice.

The seat of your problem
Lies in walking on ice.
You should try not to land
In a way that's not nice.

Had you just known ahead
You could have worn cleats,
They you might have stayed
On your feet—not your seat.

For Brenda McDowell who had just had her second child.

My dearest, darling, devoted mother
You know I love you like no other.
But, as you your silent vigil keep,
Could you just come when I CRY?
You're disturbing my sleep!

For Gail Dalton who had just announced her impending motherhood.

As teachers we've blasted the parents.
We knew what *they* did was wrong.
Considering you present condition,
Will you now sing a different song?

Later in the evening, this second poem was given to Gail Dalton.

Lest this gag should end
On one sour note
Keep those babies comin'
And you'll get our vote.

For Carolyn Krebs, school secretary, who had just been involved in a minor car accident. Her gift was a rock.

You say that bad luck haunts you,
Jumping out to give you a shock,
What you really need is insurance
Like a solid "piece of the rock."

Coach John Johnson, fourth grade teacher.

If you will hang this charm
Securely about your neck,
You'll **scare** off those other teams
And beat them all to heck!

For Wayne Smith, Oxford School Principal to accompany a gift of a package of elastic. He had scheduled a staff meeting, but as an April Fools' joke, no one showed up. For some reason, I had to walk home from school that night!

Attach one elastic
To each teacher's waist;
When it's time for a meeting
Just pull them in place.

Then they can't hide away
To do some April jokin'
You can make the meeting happen---
If the strands are not broken.

****

For the same staff dinner, I wrote these predictions for the following school year.

HEADLINE: NO SUBSTITUTE TEACHERS AVAILABLE

Sick leave for teachers is canceled
No "subs" can ever be found.
So beds will be placed in the classrooms
So teachers can teach while they're down.

The School Board has placed one restriction
On proper attire for this scene
P. J.'s and nighties must be modest
We must keep our images clean.

HEADLINE: DIVINE INTERVENTION

GOD will intervene
To make matters right;
Every teacher around
Will sprout wings overnight.

HEADLINE: SNOW DAYS AHEAD

If you gaze at the moon
And it's in the right phase,
You will be granted
ONE HUNDRED snow days.

HEADLINE: REASON FOR ROOF LEAKS REVEALED

The reason for the leaky roof
Has finally been revealed,
The bathroom plumbing was hooked up wrong
And the error deftly concealed.

At the very same time that those drops overhead
Came dripping through the ceiling,
The bathroom stools were splashing, too,--
Ugh! I have a queasy feeling!

HEADLINE: FRESH TEACHER

If you'll just cross your eyes
And then wish like crazy
You'll end each school day
As fresh as a daisy.

HEADLINE: REMARKABLE INVENTION

You will develop
A remarkable invention
Which instills instant knowledge
With 100% retention.

HEADLINE: BABY BOOM POSSIBLE

If the winter is long
And freezing and cold,

17

Many students will be added
To our little "fold."

HEADLINE: FEDERAL FUNDS CUT

Funds have been cut to the limit
Our aides should be all gone,
But a rich man dies in our town
Which allows us to carry on.

His will stipulates that our wages
Based on our trips through the halls.
Now they can race up and down just like
yo-yos
Eager to answer to our calls.

HEADLINE: ETIQUETTE IMPROVES

As sure as the clouds
Hang over the trees.
All children will suddenly
Start to say please.

HEADLINE: TEACHERS MAKE CLEAN
SWEEP WITH INNOVATIVE PLAYGROUND
EQUIPMENT

The playground now
Is well equipped,
The ponies are in the stable.

The Porta Johns
Are all in place;
It isn't just a fable.

The teachers are
All pitching in
To sanitize facilities,

They're accepting it all
With very good grace
Exercising their *best* abilities.

HEADLINE: PRINCIPAL GETS HIGH

When warm winds do blow
And a streak flashes by,
Recognize it as a Goldwing—
Mr. Smith's flying high.

HEADLINE: SURVIVAL

Next year you'll see
Nineteen-eighty three
(You ain't gonna die or nuthin'.)

HEADLINE: SHIP ARRIVES

Your ship will come in—
EMPTY!!!!

HEADLINE: STRANGE WEATHER AHEAD

As sure as the cow
Jumped over the moon,
Summer will come in January
And last until June!

****

At church I was asked to write a poem to accompany a Christmas gift of a money tree for
Rev. Dan Motto on behalf of the congregation of the Oxford, Indiana Methodist Church.

CHRISTMAS 1982

Dear Dan,
Contained hererin are just some seeds
And a bit of ...'dirty money.'
The combination may seem strange,
Or even downright funny!

But Christmastime is here again
With its spirit of love and giving,
And we naturally thought of you, dear
Dan,

Whose theme is fruitful living.

What better gift could we give to you
Than a few small seeds to grow?
For you to capture with your lens
All the beauty they will show?

The money just might buy some film.
Another button, or a tie.
Spend it as you like, dear Dan,
You're exactly our kind of guy.

****

The following poems were written for John Johnson who also taught fourth grade. At pep sessions held before important basketball games, it was his habit to read inspirational poems to the entire student body to set the right tone for the ensuing event.

I gave him a book with blank pages except for the ones I filled with these poems. I titled the book:

THE BOOK OF JOHN
(Advice for winning the game.)

If you are seeking a poem
To inspire an Oxford team,
Choose one with graphic examples
To help realize their dreams.

Try one enclosed in this volume
With words that carry some clout.
If poetry, alone, won't inspire them,
You can always kick them out!

(Begin every pep session with advice to the players via the cheerleaders.)

Rickity, rackity, rah, rah, rah!
Ole Coach Johnson sure is tall.
You'd better do what he decrees
Or he'll knock you in the nose
With one of his knees.

To really inspire your team,
To play a winning game,
It's the smart little tricks you learn about
That will bring to Oxford its fame.

So listen well to me, your coach
And follow my advice.
Games can't really be won by playing fair
Or being too nicety-nice.

Learn to surprise your opponent,
Catch him when he is off-guard,
A jab to the eye should do the trick—
Providing you do it hard.

Then there's the toe, that sneaky toe,
That can do so much for us,
Use it slyly to trip them up;
It's sure to create a fuss.

Use your elbow for poking ribs
Or punching in the back,
Don't get caught while you're doing this
Or I'll give you a thumping whack.

The secret, my lads and lasses,
To keep your moves discreet,
Remember these things I'm teaching you

And our success will be complete!

If the "ref" calls a foul for one of these
tricks,
It will be a crying shame,
I'LL DENY I TAUGHT IT TO YOU
AND YOU'LL GET ALL OF THE BLAME!

If parents are giving you a rough time because you're not letting *their superior child star*
play enough, have the cheerleaders do this yell just for them:

Johnson! Johnson!
He's our coach!
He's the mostest
With the most!

Sit down! Shut up!
Parents all
YOU ain't playin'
This game of ball!

If all else fails, you can always ask for divine intervention.

Heavenly Father, give me the strength
To coach just one more game,
Endow my team with the prowess
To prolong our winning fame.

Oh, Lord, I'm just a poor teacher.
I'm coaching the best that I can,
If my methods have offended
I pray Thee,

Strike me down…

Right here…
Where I stand.

*John—don't read this part aloud. Just act
it out!*

*Clutch your heart,
Sit down quickly,
Slump over.*

Leona M. Smith
May 19, 1983

****

Our school secretary, Mary Louise Copas, retired at the end of the 1982-83 schoolyear with
thirty-three years of faithful service to her credit. I was asked to write this poem. I read it
to the entire student body at an assembly in honor of this occasion.

OWED TO MRS. COPAS
May 25, 1983

Through the years you've seen it all
From bobby socks to jeans,

From Elvis Presley and Rock 'N' Roll
To Reagan's jelly beans.

As the only secretary we have known.
You've become an institution.
You've witnessed more than most of us;
Therefore, I submit this resolution:

Be it resolved upon this day
That you deserve a rest.

As you retire and leave us now,
We wish for you the best.

No longer must you rise and shine
When Oxford bells do ring.
You're free to *pick your poison* now,
Enjoy! And do your thing.

****

OH, RUBIK'S CUBE
1983

Oh, Rubik's Cube,
I love you much.
You've such
A tantalizing
touch.

My students
Are entranced by you.
They slight their work
And teacher, too.

I may as well
Be on the shelf,
But, that wouldn't be all
bad--
I have a Rubik's Cube,
myself!

****

For some unknown reason I tried to write a two-stanza poem that actually told a story.
Here it is.

MISCONCEPTION
1983

Ill-born,
Ill-bred,
Ill-used,
Ill-spent.

Heart-torn,
Forlorn,
Disillusioned,
Hell bent.

****

Written for Marcia (Hubler) Chinn to commemorate her winning of the Edgar P. Williams
Award for outstanding teaching (5 -27-83).

A SPECIAL KIND OF TEACHER
1983

It takes a special kind of teacher
To work with a "special" kid
To accept and understand him
Yet refrain from blowing your lid.

It takes a special kind of teacher
To be honored by her peers,
To accept her teaching assignment
And grow throughout the years.

Today we offer your *just desserts*
To symbolize your feat,
Heavenly hash and Oreos

To make your honor complete.

* * * *

My husband and I were driving to Washington, Pennsylvania to see my sister, Jennivee (Heramb) Houston. This was a letter to our daughter Lori Lynn Smith, who was a student at Indiana University at that time.

THE TRIP TO AUNTIE RED'S

My dearest darling Lori Lynn
This is your mother on this end.

Our trip began with freezing rain
As day came dawning once again.
Breakfast at Malarkey's was the best
With pancakes, bacon, and all the rest.

The highway glistens like rain-slick glass
But we chuckle at road signs as we pass,
Somehow they've sprouted overnight
With long icicle whiskers placed just right.

(This is serious stuff—hold on.)

The darkened trees stand silent in their dormant state
Keeping their winter vigil since spring is coming late.
The muddy stubbled fields lie fallow in the gloom
As rolling rain clouds encase them in their tomb.

(It's a pretty dreary day I'd say.)

We passed three graves which sparked a tale from Dad.
It certainly was creative and really not too bad.
It seems one Joshua Bennett with his team of horses four

Met a mishap at that spot; three horses were no more.

So sad and grievous was the man that he planted them right there.
Erecting those stone sentinels, his generous sorrow to share.

At midmorning we find that we have passed into the state of 'O-HI-O.'
But golly gee and holy Ned, it's just like home, you know.
Seems we ain't seen nuthin' that we ain't seen before.
But we *do* know one thing for sure, it's raining more and more.

But now we're veering to the right into the exit lane,
We'll dive into McDonald's to escape that bloomin' rain.

In the far horizon, we see West VA ahead.
The raining now has ceased but the fields still look all dead.
Hooray and hallelujah, the sun is shining bright,
As we approach your Auntie Red's
Where we will spend the night.

Auntie Red is looking old, her red hair is faded—dim.

Charley (Jennivee's husband) looks about the same
But his face has now grown quite thin.

Butch (their son) rises like a mountain growing in their midst.
And Muffie (their dog) jumps all over us begging to be kissed.

So then we talk and eat, and talk and talk some more.
Then, before you know it, they walk us to the door.

And now the sun was shining, it is warm, and hinting SPRING!
Soon rain clouds gathered over head and began to do their thing.

We drove and drove and drove and drove through all that pelting rain.
By the time we came to Oxford, it was winter once again.

Lest you feel disheartened and feeling this is a tale of woe,
We *did* have a vacation and we did go, go, go!

I guess the moral of this tale is, never sit and wait.
When you have a short vacation, be ready at the gate.

And *never* let the weather ever make you frown;
Just laugh at it! Don't let it get you down!

****

A few weeks before Halloween in 1985, the Oxford School staff where I taught for 27 years decided to have a drawing for a secret Mystery Pal. Each Pal would send a gag gift (anonymously, of course) sometime before HALLOWEEN. My Secret Pal was Pam Tabert. Along with her gift I sent an all-white card with embossed ships sailing on the sea. This was the poem I wrote to accompany the card.

A DO-IT-YOURSELF HALLOWEEN
1985

These ghost ships sail the murky sea
In search of mystery pals like me.
Because my creative mind is a blank,
It's you, my dearie, I'll have to thank.
So add a witch and a goblin or two
That will scare your socks right off of you.

After you've conjured a spectral scene
Put me in and paint me green,
Because I'm green with envy, *a prankless gal*
And *you* got stuck with *me!*
Some mystery pal!

In 1985 kindergarten teacher Pam Dalton and I decided to team up and create our own Christmas greeting cards. She would do the art work and I would write the greetings. The following poems were my contribution.

CHRISTMAS GREETINGS
11-11-85

We're sending to you
Along the way
A wish for a merry
Christmas day.

When all your fondest
Dreams come true,
To bring you joy
In all you do.

I think these lines are the best lines I have ever written and in my annual Christmas letters, these are always the words with which I close each one.

A CHRISTMAS WISH
11-10-85

May the joys of this season embrace you,
May gratitude charmingly grace you,
May the warmness of friendships caress you,
May God in his firmament bless you.

HOPE SANTA COMES TO YOUR HOUSE
11-11-85

Hope Santa comes to your house
And fills your stocking to the top.
You did sit down and write to him?
If not he may not stop!

Oh, well, perhaps old Santa
Will take pity in the end,
But, if by chance, he should forget,
Remember *we* are still your friends.

****

One of the kindergarten teachers asked me to write a poem for Mrs. Fultz, her teacher's aide, to accompany a gift from her class to Mrs. Fultz at the end of the 1986 school year.

THAT'S WHO
1986

WHO helps our teacher,
Every day?
WHO helps us work,

Or sometimes play?
WHO always
Makes our papers ready?

WHO does teacher say
    Is steady?
WHO is this

Kindly helpful WHO?
She's Mrs. FULTZ!
    That's WHO, that's WHO!

At Christmas that year, I drew Joetta Feuer's name and became her Secret Santa. Joetta taught second grade. Her husband always had to dust the top of their refrigerator because she was too short to reach it. I gave her a dusting wand.

THE DUSTY REFRIGERATOR TOP
1985

No longer must you
mutter,
"But I can't reach the top!"
Unreasonable excuses
Will simply have to stop.

Take no guff from giants.
Solve the matter quick.
Speak very, very softly.

Then BUST them with this stick!

Also in 1985, students and staff dressed as book characters in observance of National Book Week. I wanted to dress as the old woman who could tell fortunes in *Blackbird Pond*. I wrote this poem to deliver in front of the whole student body. From the information I gave them, they would have to guess what book character I represented; however, as the designated day approached, my husband who was the principal and also my boss said he would rather I wouldn't do it. So I became Pinocchio instead, but I always regretted never having gotten to do the poem. I had planned to do it with a phony, lilting, foreign accent. So now you know my side of the story so here it is.

BLACKBIRD POND

I luf to seeng and dance and play
But mostly I jost r-r-read and r-r-read all-
day.
I r-r-read sum books and stories, too,
I luf to r r read and r r r cad, don't you?

I r-r-read your palm,
Or maybe some cards.

I weel r-r-read anytheeng.

I eefen weel r-r-read a fine crystal ball
And zat, my cheeldren, iss not quite all,
I r-r-ead zee label on peekle jars,
Zee baks uf your shoes and choc-co-lat
bars,

Zee soap in zee bathtub, Zee printing on
plates
I jost r-r-read so-o-o moch
Zat sometimes I'm late.

(Repeat the first verse.)

Following the poem, as a good teacher should, I had planned to pose the following questions:

Vat vas I doink?

a. Vas I seenging?
b. Vas I song seenging?
c. Vas I seenging reading?

d. Vas I reading seenging?
e. Vas I seeng songing?
f. Vould you r-r-rather ask your teacher?

****

For the whole month of December preceding Christmas the entire staff signed up to bring in treats for the teachers' lounge. I usually wrote a poem to accompany mine.

PEANUT BRITTLE ETIQUETTE
1985

Eat it with gusto,
With care caution, with care,
And if you wear dentures,
Then *please* do beware!

A lawsuit for Christmas
Would be out of sight,
So feel free to *suck* slurpingly
Each dainty bite!

TURTLE TALE
1986

A turtle is only
A creature small.
He's not very long
And he's not very tall.

He has never been honored
Or revered you may say,
But believe me, He's talked of
On many a day.

"You're as slow as a turtle!"
Has often been said
To inject us with vigor.
With anger, or dread.

But he colored our language!
And I think you'll agree
That he left his mark
On both you and me.

(So will these turtles that I made.)

****

Each Christmas I sent individual rhymes to each child who had been kind enough to remember his third grade teacher with a small gift. Each thank you began with these words:

Christmastime has come and gone
And it's thankful I must be
For the many thoughtful little gifts
My students gave to me.

I added a special thank you for the specific gift I had received from each child.

Christmas 1985:

For Annette Watkins:

I really like your little cross
All shiny bright with pearls.
I shall always think of you, Annette,
As an *especially thoughtful girl.*

For Jessica Bruner:

I really liked your little bear
With the chalkboard right behind,
When I hang him on the tree,
The name, Jessica, will come to mind.

For Emily Cochran:

I really liked your little girl
With the chalkboard right behind,
When I hang him on the tree,
The name, Emily, will cross my mind.

For Deidre Meihls:

I really like the little horse,
The cat and candy, too,
They will always remind me of one great girl
And, Deidre, she looks like you!

For Jeffrey Wettschurack:

I liked the tissue box,
Especially since you made it!
I would give you an A-plus, plus
If I was asked to grade it.

For Andrew Brost:

I really liked the jelly jar
And what was in it, too,
I liked the way the label announced
'From the Kitchen of young Andrew.'

For Clint Barnard:

I really liked the needlework
You kindly gave to me.
Now, if I hang it on the wall,
I'll have an… all-year Christmas tree!

For James Hawkins:

I really liked the pendant
With the frog and lilies, too.
And, now, when I wear it,
I will always think of you.

For Billy Stovall:

I really liked the candle
In its holder made of glass,
It will always be a reminder
Of Bill who was in my class.

For Ronnie Glotzbach:

I really like the needlework
You kindly gave to me.
I shall hang it on the wall
For everyone to see.

For Tonya Waddle:

I really liked the needlework
That kept you sewing late,
For one so young to work so hard
Made me feel great, just GREAT!

For Tracy Smith:

I really liked the calendar
With monkeys on each page,
I'll leave it at school for *all* to enjoy,
It should be quite the rage.

For Jason M. Smith:

I really liked the stationery,
It has a fine design,
I know it will be nice to have
When I need to drop Jason M. a line.

For Jessi Lemming:

I really liked the chocolates.
I hid them in the freezer.
If Mr. Smith should want a treat,
I can offer him a sure "pleaser."

For Nicki Gregory:

I really liked the little wreath
So lacy and so white,
It will always hang on our Christmas tree
To brighten up each Christmas night.

Christmas 1986

Andrew Brost:

I really liked the needlework,
It's such a friendly sight.
I think that I will cherish it
Forever and one night.

Jason Smith:

I really liked the teddy bear
Whose candle lit the night;
When I put a match to him
He was such a friendly sight.

Cassie Barnard:

I really liked the candy
And the box that it was in;
It sweetened up the holidays
But now I'm not so thin.

Patricia Dwenger:

I really liked the dainty star
So nicely made of lace.
I hung it on our Christmas tree.
It was a perfect place.

John Cooper:

I really liked the Santa's sleigh.
With candles red and bright,
'Twas such a lovely thing to see
When I lit it up at night.

Name unknown:

The Santa and the reindeer,
Are as clever as can be.
I am so delighted
That you gave them both to me.

Kurt Anderson:

I really liked the mini-lamp,
Its candle shone so bright
That I was very tempted
To let it burn all night.

Teresa Doyle:

I really liked the dainty towels,

The ones you gave to me.
I used them for the holidays,
So all of our guests could see.

****

SHOWERS AND SHENANIGANS

"Blessings on thee, little…"

We celebrated, showered,
And applauded
Additions to the families of our staff;
Although the gifts have long
Been forgotten
There were many grand gatherings
And laughs.

In the spring of 1987 it seemed that about half of the ladies on our staff were expecting additions to their families. Following are some of the poems I wrote to accompany the shower gifts I gave.

DOUGLAS SUTTON IS HIS NAME
(For Leslie Sutton 3-2-87)

Douglas Sutton is his name.
We are very glad he came.
Time will tell what he will be
When he grows up, I think he'll
be_____

Time will tell what he will do,
Perhaps he'll turn out just like you.
Now you have your baby boy,
We hope he'll bring you lots of joy.

Vickie Pearl

THE MAKING OF A PEARL
(For Vickie Pearl 4-2-87)

Now a pearl is a pearl
And a kid is a kid;
But a kid who's a Pearl!
Just flips my lid.

I've seen many wonders
In my day and time,
But oysters have pearls
Even in rhymes.

Although I'm not
brilliant,
I do have some smarts;
Someone in this drama
Is playing the wrong
part!
(Vickie was not amused!)

ADVICE TO SHOWER EXPERTS
(For Rita Abbott 4-15-87)

We really are quite good at this,
This baby shower thing,
So wrap the gifts up and finish your cup
Before the bell does ring.

Mind you manners and don't gulp big
On this day that we honor Rita;
But do keep the action moving along
For we still must honor Juanita.

ADVICE TO AN UNBORN CHILD
(For Juanita Wagner 4-23-87)

Blessings on thee little one,
Whose precious life has just begun,
There you are, all tucked away
Safe in mommy's tum all day.

Free to flip and poke and push
And be as active as you wish;
Take heed of this advice, my dear,
Are you listening? Do you hear?

Though mommy loves you like no other,
You must never pinch your mother.

If you ever want a brother,
NEVER EVER PINCH YOUR MOTHER!

Of all of the poems I have ever written, the previous one is my very favorite.

YOU'RE ONLY A KID

A Special blessing for this child
Whose mother's manners seem so mild.
Do be cautious, little one,
Because your mother likes her fun.

She does seem pleasant in every way,
But there will come that one strange day
When all her devilish tricks erupt!
Expect the change to be abrupt.

She'll change from a caring, loving
mother
And in her place will stand another.
Her eyes will roll and snap with glee
Then you shall see, child, you shall see.

We pray you're blessed with talent and
wit;
To outfox her, you'll need every bit
Our hopes are on you--you're our best
bid,
But do be careful, you're only a kid!

****

This next poem was written for Bill Barnard, one of Oxford School's custodians, whose cow, Annie, was expecting a calf, at the same time that several of the female teachers were also "expecting." We gave him a "calf" shower. It was a lot of fun.

AN "UDDER" SAD TALE

"There's one other shower
You all must attend,"
Announced old Bill Barnard
With his famous old grin.

"So you say you're expectin'?
What's so new about that?
We're expectin' at our house
And my wife? She ain't fat.

"Once it's been done,
 That's the way it will be,
We're sure 'nuff expectin,'
My wife and me.

"There's to be a new young'n
At our house, you see.
But it won't look like her
And it won't look like me.

'Cause, there's one small detail
Ya mighta been missin'
When this one arrives
There'll be no huggin' and kissin'."

"You'd be downright slobbered on
From your head to your toes
For the one we're expectin'
Is a calf, doncha know?"

Now old Bill Barnard
Is a fine young man
But, when he spreads "bull"
Ya better duck if ya can.

Some folks tell whoppers,
Some downright lie
Bill spreads as much "bull"
As he thinks you will buy.

Yes, there'll be one more, shower
For his wobbly old calf.
This time around,
We'll have the last laugh.

(This poem was never presented to Bill
because I had another idea which follows
that we really did present to him.)

THE CALVING CLOTHES
(For Bill Barnard 5-25-87)

Every young farmer
Who is soon to be "dad"
Should strive to look dashing
And be properly clad.

For, Annie, the cow,
As Heaven only knows,
Wants nothing but the best
In New Age Calving Clothes.

Calvin Klein's Calving Clothes
Are positively divine
And, on you as mid-wife,
They would certainly look fine.

But Calvin Klein's are such a rage
That stores can't stock enough,
And Mr. Smith is so down to earth
He thought he'd call their bluff.

The price of those was way too high,
What a lot of bosh!
We'll start a new fad on our own
And give the lad OSHKOSH!

Now Bill can prance and dance about
And strike a daring pose
As he helps Annie deliver her calf
In his OSHKOSH CALVING CLOTHES!

****

As a teacher I was usually well organized enough that I could plan a whole year's instructional movies at one time. A separate form had to be filled out for each movie. I usually scheduled about one film a week. In the spring of 1987 I duly filled out my forms for each film I wanted to show during the 1987-1988 schoolyear. After spending all of that time, my forms were sent back to me stating that the forms had changed. I would have to fill out new forms. I WAS LIVID! To say the least! I sent the following poem to them.

ON BEING AHEAD OF THE GAME
1987

The game of life is strange, indeed
It throws such awful curves!
For once, I was truly ahead of the game,
Then you changed your forms!

WHAT NERVE!

A whole year of orders
I had duly made out,

Completely filled out-- except for the dates,
So it's truly with dread and an aching head
That I say—

HECK! Those NEW forms can wait!

Leona M. smith
Oxford Elementary School

P.S. It's a shame we're not both playing in the same inning! Ha!

****

In 1987, the Fleetwood Furniture Company of Holland, Michigan purchased the rights to a cabinet I had designed to store bulletin board materials—the Display Away. This is me with the President of Fleetwood, Frank Newcomb.

****

One day during the last recess, my student teacher, Tami Davis, asked me to write a poem that she could use as a writing lesson which the students could also illustrate with simple drawings. It is one of my favorite poems. I have used it in sympathy cards, get well cards, graduations, and numerous other occasions.

RAINBOW MAGIC
(For Tami Davis, May 1987)

If I could do magic,
Ya know what I'd do?
I'd tip over a rainbow
And make it smile for you.

33

After school that evening I tried to improve on the preceding poem with this version.

When I am sad
I try to see
The whole wide world
Smiling at me.

I imagine a rainbow
Then give it a shove,
The wind blows it over
And...it's smiling above.

TAMI DAVIS, STUDENT TEACHER
(For Tami Davis, May 1987 when she finished her student teaching.)

Did you really think
That you could escape
The action of my pen?

As students come
And students go,
You're the very best.

I'll write it once
And even twice
And, then, perhaps again.

So, fly on home
And pamper yourself,
You deserve a rest.

****

Our school superintendent, Mr. Vivian Simmons, was retiring at the end of the 1986-1987 schoolyear. In trying to write a poem for him, I came up with this one which was never read by anyone but me and my husband, Wayne A. Smith. Mr. Simmons loved to play golf.

BLESSINGS ON THEE, GENTLE MAN
1987

Blessings on thee, gentle man,
With clubs in cart,
Nine iron in hand,

Think of all the good you would do
If you would just shovel a ditch or two;
You still could use that nine iron thing
And dig some each day

As you retire and clear the way
For playing golf most every day.

To perfect your swing.

Here is another poem that I wrote at my husband's request but, unfortunately, it broke my heart when he refused to read it at Mr. Simmons retirement party.

MR. SIMMON'S DILEMMA
OR Mr. Simmon's Lemon
1987

For years we've known this Man as "Viv"
To some, he's V. A. Simmons;

Why has he shunned that "V" name so?
Could it be that he thinks it's a lemon?

Let's project forward to many years hence
When "Viv" should enter Heaven;

We know he should grace The Master's place;

He always rolled a seven.

When roll call starts, will he depart?
As St. Peter shouts, "VIVIAN SIMMONS?"
Will he deny that he's that guy?
Will he still think his name is a lemon?

****

MOM'S DILEMMA
For Lori Smith, 4-26-87

"I'm sending you announcements,"
Our younger daughter said,
"Could you get them in the mail
Since I never see my bed?"

Of course her mom's dilemma
Was compounded by the number
'Cause she hadn't sent enough;
Now I am missing slumber.

(Following is the note I sent to a few of my siblings and friends. I did the same for my husband's people.)

When all of us were little,
We always had to share,
So would you try one more time
And do it with a flair?
Lori will appreciate it.
Please share this epistle
with_____.

Note: This ploy worked and almost all family members were duly informed of Lori's impending graduation from Indiana University.

Lori, Leona, and Wayne Smith

LORI'S GRADUATION
June 1987

It's graduation time again
And time to honor Lori,
Time to hover over her
And shower her with glory.

Time to consider the many fine things
That she will encounter ahead;

The most important one we know
Will emerge when she goes to bed.

Never more must she buy a book
To keep at her bedside table;
At work she'll have the pick of the lot--
She'll read as many as she is able.

****

The following poem was written for Mary Flook's second child's baby shower. Mary was a member of the Oxford School Staff.

TYLER, TOO

Another blessing
Another child;
At first little Tyler will be wild.

As the new baby grows,

You'll need to tend to it,
Tyler may be jealous a bit.

Think of the new one
In all you do;
But do remember TYLER, TOO.

****

The following poem was written as a thank you to Amzi and Elma Belle Toops after we had visited them at MARQUETTE MANOR, a retirement home in Indianapolis, Indiana (June 1987). Elma Belle had been a kindergarten teacher at the Oxford School.

THANKS FOR THE DAY
1987

We'd like to be clever and witty,
Compose a most eloquent ditty,
But poets we ain't
And our words would seem quaint,
So thanks for our day in the city.

CHRISTMAS THANK YOU POEMS FOR 1987

DEIDRE MEIHLS:
You sailed in like a Santa
With your crunchy peanut brittle;
Now we're stuffed so full of it
That we're bulging around the middle.

We loved it!

HEATHER BELL:
I really liked the center piece;
It's a lovely sight to see.
I placed it on the fireplace mantle
To keep it close to me.

KELLI HOUSTON:
I really liked the broom with bells
And hung it on the wall;
I hope that it will be secure
And never ever fall.

BECKY WINCHESTER:
I really liked your little gift,
The Merry Christmas greeting,
It makes me think of a big wide smile
When you and I are meeting.

CHRIS RUTLEDGE:
I really liked your chocolates
And I know that they liked me.
For they are stuck around my middle now
For all the world to see.

JASON COLLINS:
I really liked your cookies
And the box that they were in;
They sweetened up the holidays
But now I'm not so thin.

TRACY MESSNER:
Your little basket filled with treats
Was wonderful to see,
But now the basket is empty

And the sweets are all in me!

NICK DECKARD:
I really liked the candles
They brighten up the night;
I never really ever smelled
Such a pretty sight!

DAVID STONEHOUSE:
I really liked your coffee cake
'Twas beautiful to see,
But now that little coffee cake
Has become a part of me!

TRAVIS SHERER:
I really loved the coffee cup
Which proclaimed me World's best
teacher!
You are learning early, little one,
That flattery is an A+ feature!
(Footnote; Travis, if you should ever
happen to read these rhymes, I have had
Coffee from that very cup that you gave
to me in 1987 several times each week.
Today, as I write this, it is now February 2,
2001.)
P.S. Now more time has passed—today,
as I type this again, it is August 10, 2015!

BETH BUCHANAN:
I really liked the cinnamon tree
And the clever basket heart;
I think that you and your mother, too,
Are smart when it comes to art!

JOSH FREY:
I really liked your little gift,
The candle was just right,
When I lit it Christmas Eve,
It brightened up the night.

KEILLIE CARLSON:
I really liked the Christmas towel,
The one you gave to me
I put it out on Christmas Day
For all our guests to see.

GARY LORD:
I really liked your little gift,
The basket with the wreath,
I'll make my thanks a short one
For the basket, too, was brief.

KRAIG JONES:
I really liked your little gift,
The perky candle bear,
I put him on the fireplace;
He looks so-so-so cute up there!

TIM KENNEDY:
I really liked your little gift
Proclaiming ABC;
I am the one who is the teacher,
So why are you teaching me?

KATE SCHEURICH:
I really liked your potpourri,
It smells like fine perfume

I always know just where it is
When I walk into the room.

CASEY SCOTT:
You gave some hearts, dear one,
Hanging from a wreath;
How anyone could be so nice
Is quite beyond belief.

MANDY BARRIER:
It was "love at first sight, Mandy, my love,
When I saw your Santa pup,
He seemed so very much like you,
I just had to hang him up.

ANDREW CAIN:
I really liked the Coupon Pac,
It's a gift I shall adore;
Coupons save me money
And now I can save more.

KAREN TARTER:
I really loved the basket—
The "holders" too, were great;
I'm anxious now to use them both-
Like the kids, I just can't wait.

****

In December 0f 1987 I was Secret Santa for Christie Doyle. I gave her a roll of aluminum foil. I wrote the following rhyme to accompany it:

> Foil comes in a coil,
> Can be used to boil or broil.
> Saves oil by protecting from soil,
> Best gift for a 'goil' according to Hoyle,
> Therefore: for Doyle.

****

I wrote this for one of my daughters in 1988. I think it was for Lori, but I am not sure.

THE EGGLESS WONDER,
A Birthday Cake
1988

I really dreamed about this cake.
What a wondrous creation I would bake!
Until I went to the store,
Then my expectations were no more.

I found the perfect cake for you
Only Angel Food would do.

But no fluffy frosting could be found
That I could swirl and curl around.

So, here is my offering;
It's the best I could beg--
But it still isn't wonderful—
It still lacks one egg.

****

One day in May 1988, as I left the school building and was going down the sidewalk toward my car, I spied a huge morel mushroom. It was a well-known fact that my husband and I loved to go mushroom hunting. The season usually began close to the end of April and often extended into May. The mushroom I saw on this particular day surpassed most of the ones that we had ever found. On closer examination, it turned out to be a ceramic mushroom. Later, my husband and I found the guilty party who had "planted" it. It was my teachers' aide, Karen Tarter. Luckily, we were able to find some of the same type, but smaller in height, which we "planted" in an appropriate spot. The following poem commemorates the event.

Oh, little mushroom,
How we tried
To slice you open
And get you fried.

Some smart prankster
Will be surprised
For there were more
Than he surmised.

One good laugh
Deserves another--
We also found
That mushroom's
brothers!

****

TIM AND LISA'S WEDDING REHEARSAL DINNER

On July 2, 1988, my daughter Lisa married Timothy Brakel. The rehearsal dinner was held Friday July 1, 1988 at the Morris-Bryant Restaurant in Lafayette, Indiana. All of the following thank you poems were read aloud after the dinner by the bride and groom for each of the bridal party members and the parents. Each person received a card which contained a copy of their poem.

LORI SMITH, Maid of Honor

We'd like to thank you, Lori,
For witnessing this feat;

We're doing no more measuring
So stop squirming in your seat.
If we could measure all your worth,
No measuring tape would do it,

Suffice it to say, we love you loads—
Oh, dear, I think we blew it.

ANNE TOKARZ, Bridesmaid

Anne, My Room Mate, you're the one
Who has witnessed all of our plans;
If you will "witness" one more time,
You'll have us off your hands.

We'll treasure all of the things you've done
To make "our day" complete;
We'll say farewell and thank you.
You've been so very sweet.

RUTH LEAK, Bridesmaid

Without you, Ruth, we never could
Have finalized our plans,
For coming through when we needed you,
We think you're simply grand.

When we needed a bath or a "back yard path"
You offered you offered yours to us;
We'll thank you now and take our bow
And hope there's no more fuss!

MARTHA SMITH, Bridesmaid

Our thanks to you kind Martha
For sharing in our day,
You've made it much more memorable
In each and every way.

Even though you are very shy,
You have done this thing for us;
Stop and think whom you did it for--
Ain't we worth the fuss?

BETTY HARRIS, Bridesmaid

We'd like to thank you, longtime friend,
Betty Harris Hoaks,
You and your kin have always been
Mighty neighborly folks.

We've shared together the good times;
We've also shared the bad.
Ain't you pleased that this one
Makes you feel so downright glad?

MARY SAXON, Vocal Soloist

(Mary had sung in a recital a few days
before the wedding and was so hoarse
that she couldn't perform at the wedding,
but the poem had already been written
so Lisa presented it, anyway.)

We'd like to thank you, Mary.
Your music thrills the soul
'Tis blest we are and lucky
To have cast you in that role.

How many couples who marry
Can truly say with ease,
That God reached and touched them
With such marvelous tones as these.

TOM SAXON, Organist

Our thanks to you, Tom Saxon,
For performing to perfection,
And serving as a liason
With the solemn church connection.

For impending religious rituals
Your music sets the scene
And all events that follow
Are as parts of a synchronized dream.

MICHAEL STARRS, VOCALIST

Our thanks to you dear Michael,
For traveling so far;

In our book of memories,
You'll always be a star.

We really do appreciate
Your kind consideration;
We hope you'll land that Broadway role
And start a conflagration!

LORI SNODGRASS McKINNEY, Wedding
Book Registry

In you we have another friend
Whose friendship spans the years;
Whose wit and humor have entertained
When we laughed till it brought on tears.

We're sure you'll handle our wedding
With confident ease and grace;
All who enter the church tomorrow
Should have a smile upon their face.

KEITH BRAKEL, Best Man

We'd like to thank you brother,
For being our best man.
When it comes to expert billing,
Top that, if you can!

But, on the other hand, we think
A groom outranks best man;
That is, of course, unless Emily Post
Comes up with a better plan!

MIKE WENZEL, Groomsman, Usher

We'd like to thank you, Mike,
For all the things you've done;
You've been a very helpful friend
We've had a lot of fun.

We appreciate your kindness
In witnessing our day
Perhaps some time in the future,
It's a debt I'll have to repay.

LOU VILDIBILL, Groomsman

We'd like to thank you, Lou,
For walking down the aisle
And adding to festivities
With the grandeur of your smile.

When you are walking that last long mile
And singing your last single song
It surely helps a great deal
To have a friend along!

MIKE WALKER, Piano Soloist

"Fruitcakes" sometimes marry;
Right now that is the case.
Tomorrow we're being repackaged,
We'll reside at the Brakel place.

Although we'll solemnly swear
To love and honor each other,
There will always be a special niche
For a special little brother.

BUTCH GRIMES, Vocal Soloist

A special thanks to you, Butch,
For sharing in our day,
You've helped to make it special
Much more than we can say.

If you are cruising through this town,
To keep a certain date,
Do stop in and see us;
That little gal can wait!

TONY EFFINGER, Groomsman, Trumpet
Soloist, Member of the United States Air
Force Band

(Unfortunately, due to his Air Force
duties, Tony was not able to attend. The
poem had already been written, so here
it is.)

We'd like to thank you, Tony.
Your talents are the best,
We are very fortunate indeed
To have you as our guest.

Please give our thanks to Reagan
For letting you off today,
Since the Air Force will lack one musician,
Perhaps Reagan , himself can play!

RUSTY BRIEL, Groomsman, Trombone
Soloist

We'd like to thank you, Rusty,
For performing on "our day."
You've been a super mentor
In each and every way.
Under your tutelage I, Tim,
Have moved forward to this day;
A heartfelt thanks is due you,
It was you who showed me the way.

CHRIS LEAK, Vocalist

We'd like to thank you now, Chris,
For agreeing to sing for us;
You're truly a performer
So having you was a must.

Just don't get the giggles and blow it
As you're sometimes prone to do;
If this happens tomorrow,
Mom will throw her shoe at you!

SUSAN BRAZES, Service Attendant

A special thanks is due you,
Susan Brazes, long-time friend;
May this marriage be as our friendship
And continue without end.

As service attendant you will note
The many backstage scenes;

Consider our wedding your rehearsal
For fulfilling your own set of dreams!

JUDY GRIMES, Wedding Band Conductor

Our thanks to you dear Judy,
Your energy is astounding,
When added to your exuberance,
It's really quite confounding.

It's been a joy to have you
Conduct our wedding band,
The music was quite heavenly
Under your guiding hand.

Through the years, you've been to me,
A mentor, a mother, a friend:
You've been my inspiration;
A perfect idol to the end.

My life, I hope, will be like yours
A symphony in total;
A baton, and now a man
And a marriage that is modal.

IZETTA BRAKEL, Seamstress who made all
of the bridesmaids' gowns. (The groom's
aunt.)

We'd like to thank you, Izetta,
For jumping in so quick;
When you offered us your services,
You were our very first pick.

Your expertise at needlework
Is surpassed only by your speed,
And your kindness, and generosity
In performing this great deed.

STEVE and HOLLY RAATZ, (They were
home from Kuwait where they taught in
the American School for several years.
Lisa also taught band there for just two
years during the same time period.)

We'd like to thank you, college friends,
Steven Raatz and Holly;
A wedding day without you here
Would be a serious folly.

You add a fifth dimension
To an already joyous scene,
We are so glad to have you here
To share our ultimate dream.

MATT MUEHLAUSEN, Piano Accompanist

A heartfelt thanks is due you
For your symphony of sound.
You're one of the best musicians
That we have ever found.

We are quite pleased to have you
Share this day with us;
If time would only allow it,
We'd make a bigger fuss!

TERRI EWIGLEBEN, Trumpet Soloist

We'd like to thank you, Terri,
For performing on our day,
A most electric wedding march
In your own inimitable way.

The heraldic sound of your trumpet
We hope will command the attention
Of all of those who have gathered
For the first Smith-Brakel Convention.

DARVIN HALWES, Usher

We'd like to thank you, Darvin,
For ushering in our day
And letting those much-loved fish
Swim freely on their way.

Hunting and fishing are both great sports
That put one to the test;
Consider the "catch" I'm making now,

You must agree, she's the best!

BRENT JOHNSON, Usher

We'd like to thank you, Brent
For ushering in our day
And leaving those much-loved fish
To swim about and play.

But hundreds of days of cycling
Or fishing in the lake
Cannot compare with my Lisa,
For she's my most prized "take."

WAYNE AND LEONA SMITH, Parents of
the bride

I'd like to thank you, Mom and Dad,
For paying for this bash.
And for being so downright amiable
In supplying wedding cash.

It's really a very small price to pay
'Cause I'm giving it back, you see;
In exchange, please accept a brand new
son.
Think of him as a gift from me!

WAYNE AND ALICE BRAKEL, Parents of
the groom.

I'd like to thank you, Mom and Dad,
For paying for this bash
And being so downright amiable
When parting with your cash.

You always taught me to be fair,
Honest, grateful, and kind,
So I'm giving you a brand new daughter,
She's the best one I could find!

The next poem was printed on wide blue
ribbons which were presented to the
sixty members of Tim and Lisa's Wedding

Band which was composed of fellow
musicians, high school and college
friends, students and others. They wore
their thank you ribbons pinned to their
chests. The band played the recessional
with Judy Grimes, Lisa's college music
professor conducting.

We met,
We married,
You came,

You played.

We loved it,
We thank you,
You've now earned a grade.

No fuss, A PLUS
To you from us.

Mr. and Mrs. Tim Brakel

****

I wrote this next poem for Lisa to accompany a bachelorette party gift of an old-fashioned
chamber pot.

PARENT'S PRAYER

May the road rise up
And meet you,
May sunshine
Always greet you.

May all your days
Be as happy as this'n,
May you always
Have a pot to piss in.

Ruth (Leak) Ewigleben, Lisa (Smith) Brakel

44

Taylor Music Inc. of Aberdeen, S. Dakota repairs band instruments and publishes a newsletter. In 1988, they held a contest for poems about bands that might be used on the last page of their newsletter. Both my daughter, Lisa, and her husband, Tim Brakel, were band teachers at that time. They passed the contest entry on to me. Only the best entries would be published but the author of the very best poem would also receive a $75.00 prize. I was awarded a pair of drum sticks for participating. This is my poem.

HIS BAND
1988

'Twas the night before contest
When all through the school,

All the teachers had left
Except for one fool.

The fool was a teacher,
The one who taught band,
His schedule was heavier
Than any in the land.

But he thought it was useful,
This competition bit,
It would help all of his students
Become musical hits.

He made all of the arrangements,
Chose the music, had practice,

Till his head roared like thunder,
And his eyes prickled like cactus.

On the day of the contest
What should appear?
But judges who were deaf!
They really couldn't hear!!

They rated the band "awful"
The worst in the land!
The teacher shrugged lamely,
'Cause…well…he still…had…. HIS BAND!

For once all of the parents
Stood by his side,
"It's not your fault," they murmured—
So he still had his pride.

****

The Oxford School Staff had a surprise necktie shower for the principal, my husband, Wayne A. Smith. I wrote this and posted it on the wall in the hallway outside his office to commemorate the occasion—his birthday, September 20, 1988.

THE NECKTIE PARTY
1988

A "necktie party" was the plan
To laud Mr. Smith, our big boss man.
We gave him ties of every kind
And some that you could never find!

We now display them in the hall
To be admired (?) by one and all.

Thank goodness we live in a modern age
For "necktie parties" were once quite the rage.

HAPPY BIRTHDAY, MR. SMITH!

45

****

One member of the Oxford Staff (I have forgotten who) put a stuffed rat in another member's desk drawer hoping to scare the socks off of the recipient. A note was attached asking that person to pass it on to another. When I found it in my desk drawer, I was prompted to write the following poem and sent it on to Charlene Wilkins, Oxford School librarian.

A RAT TALE
10-21-88

Ah spied me this gruesome critter,
'N expected him tuh scurry,
He warn't movin' none a' tall,
He warn't in no big hurry.

"Whut good is he?" ah sez tuh muhself,
'But a dumb –lookin' ugly ole rat?
Ain't a one o'God's critters
Bein' as USELESS as that!"

I set muhself down tuh have a good think

As ah poured me a cup o' tea.
Jest as ah wuz addin' sum sugar
Guess whut cum tuh me?

The body o' that rat jest fit muh hand
Right purty as can be
'N' 'at lo-o-ng ole tail on 'at dumb ole rat
Stirred muh cup o' tea fer me!
    Now, ah, ax yo' God,
    Ain't cha jest a "a wee little bit"
      Kinda proud o' me?

A GREAT KID
11-10-88

Can any child be greater
Than the likes of you, my dear?
For tending to your Mommy
And always being here.

I know that if we need you,
You'll gladly heed the summons
You'll drag along your Timothy
And help will be forthcomin'.

ROBBIE HALL
11-17-88

My dear little Robbie
Thanks for the note;
It's so nice to know
That I have your vote.

Please do your work
And try to be good,
Always be as polite

As every boy should.

Then, when the time comes,
To cast my own vote
I'll shout, "I'll vote for Robbie
'Cause he wrote me a note!"
Your "great" third grade teacher,
Mrs. Leona M. SMITH

****

In November of 1988 I had an operation for a neuroma on the bottom of my foot and was laid up for a few days until I was allowed to return to school. Several of the Oxford staff members sent dishes of food home with Mr. Smith each night. Following are the thank you notes I wrote in response.

WITH HIS HANDS
11-11-88

With his own hands, he served to me
A delicious, tasty repast—
Baked potatoes with chicken and noodles
And scru-u-umptious peas in fine glass.

For dessert, he served with my coffee,
The most beautiful brownies I've seen—

So crispy and crunchy and yummy
I was tempted to lick the plate clean.

We all know who slaved in the kitchen—
It was Karen, Roberta, and Dru;
When behind one lone man stand three women
What wonders that one man can do!

A FULL HARVEST
1988

We're thankful for the harvest,
We're thankful for the fall,
And, at this time we're thankful
For the good cooks one and all.

The one who made delicious soup,
The one who made the bread,

The one who made sweet dumplings
To keep us both well fed.

Can anything be finer
Than good friends such as these?
The best thing I can think of is
Would you pass a napkin, please?

A WELCOME DELAY
11-16-88

Sausage gravy and biscuits,
Green bean casserole,
Gorgeous brownies and salad—
Dishes that thrill the soul.

We rarely have a menu
As intricate as this,
Especially on a school night,
What extraordinary bliss!

A special thanks is due you
For your culinary skills;
We'll just delay another day
Our need for diet pills!

"IT'S SPAGHETTI"
(For Karen Tartar—my teachers' aide.)
11-20-88

She said, "It's spaghetti."
He said, "No, it's not."
She said, "Tomato casserole,"
"That's what we have got."

Well, we heated it up
And gave it a try;

We stuffed ourselves full,
Then said with a sigh,

"No matter what she called it,
It's all gone—what a shame!"
But we never did agree
On its bonafide name!

OUR BLESSINGS
11-21-88

What dishes we have
seen
Prepared by such as
thee.
In payment what you get
Is another poem by me.

We really have been
blessed
By your culinary skills

If you need a Santa for
Christmas,

One of us should fill the
bill!

Thanks a million!

****

Each December, the staff at Oxford School had a sign-up sheet for bringing in treats for the teacher's lounge. I made Black Walnut Fudge and wrote this poem to accompany it.

OH, FUDGE
11-24-88

Have you ever locked yourself out
And the door just wouldn't budge?
You exclaimed disgustedly
And even quite robustedly,
            "OH, FUDGE!"

Have you tasted something awful
That you KNEW just might be sludge?
You spat it out dramatically
As you muttered, quite emphatically,
            "Oh!! FUDGE?"

Have you ever felt just like the maid
And KNOWN that YOU were the
DRUDGE?
You puddled up so tearfully
And whimpered so uncheerfully.
            "Oh, fudge!"

Have you ever opened a box of rocks
That you thought were covered with
mud?
Then someone close to you
Gave you a little nudge;
You firmly declared so knowingly
And even stated glowingly,
            "Oh...FUDGE!

****

I had a reason for writing this poem, but now I have lost the 'who' and 'why?'

MIXED SIGNALS
12-10-88

Santa missed our house last year
His reindeer flew on past,
We weren't bad or anything

So we wondered how he dast.
Then we remembered what we'd learned
In one forgotten time,

Perhaps we'd heard it once at church
Or in a nursery rhyme.

"Ask and ye shall receive" we'd been told
So we asked for a whole big lot
"But, asking isn't polite," said Mom
So Christmas requests we forgot.
So did Santa.
      Oh, well….

Now this year
If I had one wish for Christmas
I know what that one wish would be.
I'd wish for nice toys for all girls and boys
And, maybe one small one for me.
Alternate last line:
And maybe a MILLION FOR ME!
Take your pick, Santa.

****

YOU HAVE ESCAPED MY PEN
1989

Through the years
You are one of the few
Whose antics
Have escaped my pen.

Therefore, my friend,
With that in mind,
I'll engage my pen again.
P.S. Unfortunately, your name now
escapes me.

TARTER'S BEST
5-21-89

There they hung upon the wall,
They stood out from the rest.
I recognized them instantly—
They were labeled "Tarter's Best."

There really wasn't a label as such
I just thought it in my head,
But when it came, it echoed loud!
And seemed to have been said.

When Karen Tarter leaves this room,
She'll be lost way out in space
Without those desks surrounding hers
Being jammed all in one place.

So here's a peaceful supplement;
That will neither laugh nor mock,
They'll always be just where they should
Let's call them *Tarter's Flock*.

LORI WEDDLE'S GRADUATION
5-23-89

Graduation time is here
It has truly come at last.
Gone are the woes of growing up,
All of that fun stuff is past.

As you now don that cap and gown
Your *new* wings will unfurl,
Always set your goals quite high
Then stretch up and touch them, girl!

AN A+ KID (Lori Smith's birthday)
6-3-89

I am not the best of poets
And my wrapping isn't great
But when it comes to daughters,
You command an A+ rate.

A+ for all the things you are,
A+ for things you say,
By George, I think we've done it Dad!
She's A+ all the way.

YOUR FIRST ANNIVERSARY (Tim and Lisa Brakel)
6-11-89

Your first year of marriage has ended
Celebrations are now taking place,
You've accepted your new roles with
grandeur
And have fashioned your own little place.
The second year should be quite easy

The first one is always the worst—
But if things get really awful and yucky—
Then the second will be worse than the
first.
Now the third year should turn out better
And---

Oh, well, HAPPY ANNIVERSARY!

****

I sent the following poem to Rosalie Woodard and Evelyn Tosser, former high school classmates of mine who had planned a forty-first anniversary reunion for the class of 1948 from Honey Creek High School in Terre Haute, Indiana.

REUNION REFLECTIONS
7-30-89

I'd like to thank you, high school chums,
The reunion was just great.
For all the clever things you did;
You deserve an A+ rate.

And wasn't it just wonderful
To see "the kids" again?

Although we may have shed some hair
Or gained an extra chin?

Thank God we know from times long past
Personalities buried inside
You can tell from our appearance now
Life has dealt us one heckuva ride!

****

I wrote this as a possible advertisement when we were putting our Oxford, Indiana home up for sale. We didn't use the poem.

51

THE "DANDILY" HOUSE
8-1-89

I'm a house in search of a master.
Please come and take care of me.
My space is quite large
And you'd be in charge;
I would serve both of you dandily.

*****

A BIRTHDAY WISH (For Wayne Brakel)
8-15-89

Now is the time
For all good men
To rack up one more
year.

It seems that
You're among them,

So here's your wish right
here.

May both your son
And daughter-in-law
Remember you're Tim's
Dad.

And give to you
The finest day
That you have ever had.

P.S. That's called
"Passing the Buck."

****

IT'S THE SPIRIT OF THE THING

I took peanut brittle and a pecan pie to the Oxford teacher's lounge in December of 1989.
The poem explains my problems.

A hit? Or a miss?
Is it brittle or pie?
I'll know when I hear a groan or a sigh.

The brittle, I know,
Is a tiny bit brown;
The pie is quite rich

And cholesterol-bound.

Just remember it's Christmas,
That's the principle of the thing--
It's the spirit that counts—
Not the cooks or what they bring.

HAPPY BIRTHDAY, MRS. TOOPS
2-2-90

'Tis gracious you are
And kind and friendly;

Therefore, best wishes
We do send thee.

We hope your days
Are filled with bliss,

And that all your greetings
Are better than this.

****

In the summer of 1989 we spent three weeks in Florida searching for the ideal place to retire. We decided to have a home built at Scottish Highlands at Leesburg, Florida. After buying the lot we learned that Wayne's older brother had a friend who lived in that same retirement development. We spent the night in his home while we completed our arrangements. His name was Jim Reed.

THANK YOU JIM REED
1989

Jim Reed, we thank you kindly
For your hospitality;
We thought your little house
Was just as nice as it could be.

Brother Bob is doing fine
His hip has now been set;

He won't be mended for a while
Or running races yet.

We think our plans have all been made
They're the best that we can do;
We just can't wait to see our house
When the builders are all through!

****

When we retired in 1990, many of our school patrons earned our thanks. Laura Hackley was one of them. She created a beautiful doll made with raffia and lace.

YOU'RE A DOLL
1990

A little flounce,
A little lace,
A little hat
With ribbon graced.

A tiny basket
Of perfect flowers
To while away
Retirement hours.

I could not make
A doll so sweet
To give away
For another's treat!

****

The school bus drivers and custodians were kind enough to host a dinner for my husband and I at the Beef House near Covington, Indiana. It was and still is our very favorite restaurant. This was the thank you we sent each of them.

THANK YOU FOR THE DINNER
1990

One could surmise
From our very size
That eating is one of our pleasures.

None can surpass

Nor ever outclass
The Beef House's own touted treasures.

The only thing better
Is found in this letter,
It is friendship that lasts through all
seasons.

Although we're not thinner,
Many thanks for the dinner
And an evening exceedingly pleasing!

****

Wayne and Leona Smith

The teachers at Oxford Elementary were kind enough to have a retirement party for us at Bryant's in Lafayette, Indiana. They picked us up in a school bus! Of course, all of them were already on the bus. What a hoot! We gave each person who attended this thank you.

ADIEU
1990

The time has come to bid adieu
To each and every one of you;
To shake your hand with style and grace
While smiling sweetly in your face.

But you all know our reputations—
Just plain mean—no alterations;
So give us a gruff, old craggy smile,
We'll know you've sent us off in style.

54

As for us, we can finally PLAY
Until old age gets in the way;
And if it does, yes, that's a loss,
Life will STILL be better when WE are our boss!

School Board member Dave Dimmich's wife painted and presented us with a picture. This is their thank you.

PICTURE THIS
1990

A little house,
A little tree,
A little yard
For thee and me.

Picture us
Behind the wall,
Enjoying retirement
And having a ball!

Retired Curriculum Coordinator Bill Bird's wife, Marilynn, made a quillo for us.

A PILLOW? A QUILLO?
1990

A pillow? A quilt?
A quillo you say?
It can be used
In several ways?

Whatever it is,
It's deucedly clever!
Our brightest remark
Is, "Well, I never!"

Speech Therapist Drucilla McFerren made a beautiful counted cross-stitched sampler. Here is her thank you.

CROSS-STITCHED THREADS
1990

Cross-stitched threads
So neatly placed,
School mementos
Fondly graced
By such a loving,
Caring hand
Make these two Smiths
Feel mighty grand.

Another gift that I received was an Arzella blouse done in a school motif. It was from Owen York, whose mother worked in a shop that sold Arzella apparel. This was the thank you I wrote.

AN ARZELLA TREASURE
1990

An Arzella treasure
With bag, bow, and seal
Has added immensely
To the joy that I feel.

Your gift stands out
From all of the rest,
Because you cared enough
To give me the BEST!

The next poem was written for Millie and Nancy Roger's family for a basket which their mother, Renee, made. For the past 12 years, we have used that basket to hold napkins.

A TISKET, A TASKET, A WONDERFUL BASKET
1990

A tisket, a tasket,
What a wonderful basket!
What marvelous things it could hold!

From goodies to sewing

And a list that keeps growing

Tremendous possibilities unfold.

Your generosity is beguiling
With thankfulness we are smiling
For this quite thoughtful treasure we hold.

****

This poem was written for Phyllis and Lou Fell who hosted a retirement party for Wayne and I and all of our neighbors.

THE COOKOUT
7-20-90

Good neighbors, good food,
Fellowship, the best
Made these two Smiths
Feel mightily blest.

Jelly beans counted,
Bubble gum chewed,

Little black bugs
Heartily shooed.

Clouds overhead,
The rumble of thunder—
We cherish it *all*,
Till they plow us both under!

****

We sent the following poem to Dick Atha, a longtime coach in Benton County, when it was decided that the new field house would be named in his honor.

RESTITUTION
1990

No greater tribute can be paid
Than honoring one's name,
Especially when it elevates
One humble man to fame.

Congratulations to you, Dick,
No one we know deserves it more,
It's good to know, after *hundreds* of
games,
That they've finally evened the score!

****

Our daughters, Lisa and Lori, and Wayne's nieces, Betsy Stevenson and Martha Smith, helped when we finally made the move to Florida.

THE MOVE TO SCOTTISH HIGHLANDS
(At Leesburg, Florida)
July 31, 1990

Boxes stacked high,
No room to walk,
Lots to be done
As we unpack and talk.

Objects discovered
That were thought to be lost,
Some reappraised,
Then repacked or tossed.
Meals to be served
Out on the patio
And shared with our kid's
Own Mommy and Dadio.

Utilities hooked up,
Fine adjustments made,
New habits formed
For life's new parade.

Dreams realized,
Ours for the getting.
We learned the secret
For controlling life's flow—

Map it out, wisely,
Push forward and go!

CHAPTER 2
SCOTTISH HIGHLANDS
Loch Ness Court
Leesburg, Florida

Our Florida move was traumatic,
We left behind families and friends;
The many new people we encountered
Formed a quite masterful blend.

Gone were the mid-western accents,
The new regional dialects enthralled,
While one man from Maine "pahked his cah"
His wife voiced her own cute "y'alls."

Gone were the Indiana cornfields,
Gone was the ice and snow,
Replaced by the everyday sunshine
And many new people to know.

We moved to a house that we had built at Scottish Highlands, a retirement community close to Leesburg, Florida on July 31, 1990. The man who sold us our lot was a retired dentist named Tom Casto. A week or so after we moved in, he and his wife, Fran, took us out in their boat on Lake Harris. They took us down the Dead River where we saw scenes similar to those that one might see in magazines such as *National Geographic*. We went across the lake to a tiny restaurant overlooking the lake called Crackers Cove where we had breakfast. It was a most memorable experience—especially the champagne toast that preceded the breakfast. I wrote the following poem to thank them.

To the captain and his queens—
The royal hosts,
The bubbly sip,
The awesome scenes—
A MAGNIFICENT TRIP!

We'll tell you now
Just where we stand;
You've made these Smiths
Feel mighty grand.

Howard and Joanna Houghton, our new neighbors across the street had a cocktail party for us and invited all of our new neighbors. I wrote this thank you for them on August 5, 1990.

A sip of this,
A bite of that,
Toasting new friends,
Having a chat.

All prepared
By caring hands—
Sure made these Smiths
Feel mighty grand.

I wrote the following poem for our next door neighbor, Betty Pfau, in August of 1990. Wayne and I had purchased tickets to hear Joanne Castle who had played piano on Lawrence Welk's TV show for years. I came down with a terrible cold a day or two before the concert and felt that I should not attend. We had learned that Betty loved music so we asked her husband, Jack, if it would be okay for Betty to go to the concert with my husband, Wayne.

Later, I asked Betty how she liked the concert. Her reply was, "It was great!" She hesitated for a moment then added, "If you ever get tired of Pete, (my husband) I'll take him." Needless to say, that did not happen. To thank us for the concert she made us some delicious cinnamon roll-ups. Following is my thank you to her:

Your cinnamon roll-ups
Were just so great
That I must report
That we overate!

But, nevertheless,
The future looks bright—
We'd just liked to know,
Do you bake every night?

I wrote the following limericks one afternoon just for fun. They were about the neighbors. We had, by that time formed a hillbilly band led by John Carroll, a retired pharmacist and his wife, Frona, who was our MC. John hailed from Maine and Frona was from North Carolina. We only had four members who were real musicians and the rest of us were noise makers. About once a week, we performed for other retirees, and we got to know each other quite well—thus the poem about our band members.

There once was a lady named Betty
Who dined on rich sauce with spaghetti;
    She ate that good stuff
    Till she'd had enough,
So she turned it all into confetti.

There once was a golfer named Jack
Who played golf till the sun turned him black;
    He said, "That's too bad
    Since white skin I thought I had,
I'd better slip home through the back."

There once was a lady, Joanna,
Who dined on fine soup and bananas;
    Howard said "Spice it up."
    So when she next served a cup,
She dressed in a red-hot bandana.

There once was a fellow named Howard
Whose antics were always high-powered;
    He'd rip and he'd snort
    And gleefully cavort,
He just wasn't himself till he'd showered.

There once was a fellow named Don
Who ate hot dogs drenched with poupon;
    He would eat six or eight
    And they still tasted great
So he'd have some with Heinz catsup on.

There once was a lady named Toni
Who cooked up some cheese macaroni;
    She served it for brunch
    And once more for lunch
Till Don begged for some good fried bologna.

There once was an Indiana Jones
Who moved here and said, "Now I'm
home."
        "I will move nevermore,
        It's too much of a chore."
So he lived here and nevermore roamed.

There once was a lady named Barb Jones,
Who sang as she baked a few scones,
        The oven was hot
        It was burned that they got
She then sang in very high tones.

There once was a chap named John
Carroll
Who said he was over a barrel,
        If he just had more hands
        He could be his own band
And play music all day without care-o.

There once was a lady named Frona
Who served possum and wild macaroni,
        "It's more lively," she said,

"When the possum ain't dead,
Then the pasta don't look quite so
scrawny."

There once was a fellow named Frank,
Who ate his food first, then he drank.
        He thought he'd be fitter'n a
fiddle
        If he'd drink in the middle
But we thought his idea really stank.

There once was a lady named Natalie
Who said, "Over there a white cat I see,
        When I turn my back
        He changes to black,
The next time he does look quite tigerly."

There once was a fellow named Wayne
Who surveyed his outside terrain,
        If he saw a mound
        Freshly heaped on the ground
He'd clap his hands over his brain.

****

The following poem was written for neighbors Howard and Joanna Houghton for their fortieth wedding anniversary. Wayne and I hosted a celebration party for them.

FORTY YEARS
1990

Forty years of living together,
Raising kids, battling weather;
Doing all the things you should,
Like going to church and being good.

Isn't it time that you had some fun?
To sort of balance the good that you've
done?

Like kicking up your heels in Atlantic City,
Winning some loot and sitting pretty?

No! Worldly pleasures aren't your thing.
Go! Find a rare bird!
Have your fling!

I wrote the next poem for Howard Houghton after he had heart surgery. He did not like the implications I made in the poem but it is still my opinion that he was a male chauvinist.

CHAUVINISTICALLY YOURS
1990

When they have turned you inside out
What will they find inside?
It just might be that they will see
Your chauvinistical pride.

Perhaps they'll bury it within
To vanish evermore,
Or maybe they will unleash the thing
And make it worse than it was before.

Whatever happens along the way,

In the end you will see,
That if we women didn't take care of you men
What messes your lives would be,

So you'd better be kind to Joanna
As she helps you recuperate,
You're IN HER HANDS, and you CAN'T AFFORD
To be a chauvinistical ingrate.

****

For a couple of years after we moved to Scottish Highlands, I served on a committee called The Music Lovers club. Our job was to find musicians who would perform for our residents for free. I procured most of the acts and also wrote thank you poems for them.

Ron Cook was an organist from the Fletcher Music Store, at Scottish Highlands. Many of the residents bought organs from them and in exchange the music store gave them free group lessons. I was one of them.

FOR RON COOK, ORGANIST FROM THE FLETCHER MUSIC STORE
1990

From rollicking, frolicking
Toe tapping tunes,
To mighty and mellow
And grand.

You played them ALL
From beginning to end—

Even conjuring up
A big band.

We laud your great talent,
Applauding the fact
That you allowed us
To share your great act!

****

The ladies on our street took turns planning luncheons for all of us ladies. This was written for the first luncheon I sponsored. It was to Cassadega, Florida, which was a community of

61

psychics. I had seen several of these same psychics on a television show called *Sixty Minutes* many times before we moved to Florida.

I was anxious to see what it looked like—other ladies were not so anxious. In fact, one woman in our group refused to even buy a soda pop from a machine! Fortunately, I had taken a thermos of lemonade to share with the group in the middle of the afternoon while sitting beside Spirit Lake. That, too, went over like a big a thud! It was great fun for me— but not so for several in our group. (December, 1990)

GHASTLY, GHOSTLY IMAGES
1990

Ghastly, ghostly images
Will dance before your eyes;
You may see and hear about
Much more than you surmise.

Our trek to Cassadaga
Will begin at 10:15
Meet in the street with pencils

(I had prepared a quiz for them to do after the visit.)
Prepare for a scary scene.

Do remember your manners,
Think only thoughts that are kind;
Remember the psychics around you
Have been trained to read your mind.

Perhaps the invitation itself frightened them, but my philosophy is that psychics are just plain people who may or may not be psychic.

****

The Loch Ness Monsters' Band

Frank Biesinger, Howard Houghton, Jack Ptau, John Carroll and Don Kartye
Nat Biesinger, Joanna Houghton, Betty Ptau, Frona Carroll, Leona Smith, Toni Kartye

In the fall of 1990, John and Frona, who lived on our Loch Ness Court cul-de-sac, formed a hillbilly band called The Loch Ness Monsters' Band.

John played the harmonica and guitar. Frona was to be our announcer. Betty Klingerman, who lived on a different street, was a natural musician. She could play all sorts of keyboards and in the Loch Ness Monsters' Band, she played the accordion. If anyone could hum a tune, she could play it. Her husband, Wayne, played the banjo and to top off the list of real musicians, Reverend Randall Parsons played guitar and sang duets with his wife, Agnes. We performed for many church groups and retirement parks in the Leesburg area.

I wrote the following rap thinking it would be a unique way to introduce the Loch Ness Monsters at performances. John and Frona didn't seem to grasp the idea of a rap. However here it is.

LOCH NESS MONSTER RAP
1991

First we have Don
Playing the wash tub
fiddle;
He is too tall
To be in the middle.

Next there is Jack—
He doesn't scrub clothes,
He plays his washboard

But smells like a rose.

Then there is Toni—
You really should try it—
Those spoons that she
plays
Would be great for a
diet.

Next is Leona
And although she is
green,
She still can play
The tambourine.
Next we have Betty;
Those are her spoons
When she beats a
rhythm,

The young men all
swoon.

Then there is Nat--
She does scrub clothes.
She plays the washboard,
Then launders her hose.

This man is Frank—
He plays the Stump
Fiddle;
He's too dangerous
To play in the middle.

Next we have Wayne
Who plays the banjo;
He plinks it and plunks it
And strums it, you know.

Then there is Howard—
He plays the whistle;
If he blows it too hard
 It takes off like a missile.

Here is Joanna,
She loves what she plays;
She shakes and she
rattles
So step out of her way.

Now we have Agnes,
She sings or she plays,
The Monsters all miss
her
If she is away.

Beside her is Randall,
A versatile man;
He strums or he sings
And plays the saw when
he can.

Then there is Betty,
The accordion is her
thing;
If Wayne hits a bad note
She'll give back his ring.

We also have Frona—
She's from the South;
Her tambourine walks
But she runs with her
mouth.

Next we have Barb
Who plays castanets;
Do watch her closely—
She may pirouette!

Then there's Bud Jones;
The fiddle is his thing
And, boy, are you lucky!
He ain't gonna sing!

Last is John Carroll,
The leader of the band;
And you have just met
The whole Loch Ness
clan.

****

In June of 1991, there was great deal of dissension at Scottish Highlands. Various arguments were being bandied about—real or imagined faults of the Scottish Highlands developers, the Pringle family. We sent the Pringles the following poem.

People who bitch
        Are always quite visible,
They complain and destroy
        Making others quite miserable.
We want you to know
        That a few are around
Who are living quite happily
        But making no sound.

It's time that we let you
        Know just how we feel;
We are proud to live here

        And we got a good deal.
Our neighbors are the best
        Our moving here was fate.
There is no fun in living
        If one can only hate.

We worked hard and saved
        To afford our small plot.
And we're mighty proud
        Of the lifestyle we've got.
May those who complain
        And make life so miserable

64

Go elsewhere to live—
　　Make themselves invisible.

Therefore dear Pringles,

And Tom Casto, too,
We send this fond thank you
　　From our house to you.

****

HAPPY BIRTHDAY TONI
1991

When it comes to birthdays,
There's one gal on Loch Ness
Who isn't even 60 yet!
She's been cheated, that's my guess.

Look at all the birthdays
The rest of us have had;
With gifts and celebrations,
Having *more cannot be bad*.

So, Toni, child, we wish you
The best, on this, your day;
And pray that somehow you'll catch up—
Somewhere along the way.

****

The following poem was written for my sister Elva (Heramb) Hayworth.

HAPPY BIRTHDAY, ELVA
1991

The relationship of sisters
Is a somewhat fragile thing.
It's thrust on one by birth,
But what does it really bring?

We could side with each other
Against a sibling who was bad,
Or even share caring
For a mom or a dad.

We can live our own lives
The way that we please,
But share family history
Or communicable disease.

But the two of us differ
From where I stand here;
I CAN'T share your BIRTHDAY;
It's all yours, my dear.

65

HAPPY BIRTHDAY, BARBARA JONES
1991

Barbara Jones is older today
How old she is, I cannot say,
I do know she is very spritely.
And replaces batteries almost nightly.

Is there a connection? I cannot say,
But Barbara Jones is older today,
And since she is, suffice it to say,
She *really* deserves a HAPPY BIRTHDAY!!!

BETTY KLINGERMAN
1991

Betty, darlin'
You're the best;
Glad to hear
You passed your tests.

SIS-BOOM-BAH!
HIP-HIP-HOO-RAY!!!
'Twas nice that God
Said you could stay.

TIM BRAKEL, BIRTHDAY
1991

Another year.
What will it bring?
No time to listen
To ANY bird sing.

No time for movies,
No time for play

Many books and papers
Will stand in your way.

So, why celebrate?
With forecasts of doom?
'Cause some sucker at
McCutcheon

Now squirms in your
room!

So, kick up your heels!
Celebrate "32"!
There's a new life ahead
Just waiting for you.

HAPPY BIRTHDAY, LORI (Daughter)
1991

To Lori Belinski,
The cream of the crop,
We wish for you happiness
That never will stop.

We wish you success
In all that you do,
And pray HE comes quickly
To share it with you.

Perhaps HE is searching
For one such as you;
So play your cards wisely
And stay in full view.

When you blow out your candles,
Hold HIM in your mind
And pray that HIS searching
Results in a FIND!

Bud Jones had told Wayne that he had seen a deer in the woods next to our house.   He hadn't. He was lying. However, Wayne believed him and placed a block of salt in the woods for the "deer." Bud chortled with glee for ages because he had played a trick on Wayne, a former school principal, who had a degree in Animal Husbandry, while Bud had only a high school education and worked in a factory.

HAPPY BIRTHDAY, BUD JONES
1991

If we could grant one wish for you,
This is what it would be,
     We'd wish for good health
     And plenty of wealth
And a big celebration for thee!
     OR

If we could grant one wish for you,
This is what it would be,
     We'd wish for new spectacles
     Or even a receptacle
To capture a real deer for thee.

****

I was asked to write this poem to share with our neighbors at a party for Frank Biesinger.

HAPPY BIRTHDAY, FRANK (Biesinger)
1991

SEVENTY YEARS!!!!!!!!
It can't be so!
But that's what you said,
And you should know.

Consider the food
That you've stored away,
And the working and doing
That you've done every day.

Just think of the times
That you've scrubbed your skin,

It's surprising any is left
For you still to be in!

Seventy years old?
And you STILL drive a car?
You mow your own lawn?
And you've come MIGHTY FAR.

Considering the facts,
We may as well be frank
There's still some good living
Left in your "bank."

CONGRATULATIONS, LISA
1991

Daughters who return to school
Make parenting a pleasure,
It's even more of a thrill
When YOU foot the bill,

Then we know we've produced
A real treasure!
(Lisa had returned to college to get a
master's degree in Library Science.)

P.S. Congratulations are in store
As we witness A's galore,
And we'll sing praises evermore
If Tim can even up the score!

(Tim was about to start back to school to get his doctor's degree In Music Education.)

****

Randall Parsons was a retired minister from the Tavares Methodist Church in Tavares, Florida which we attended.

SORRY YOU'RE NOT UP TO PAR, PARSON PARSONS (Reverend Randall Parsons)
1991

What a pity, parson,
That you've gotten in a jam,
And have to sit so quietly
And be a Silent Sam.

We know how that must irk you
Since inactive you are not;

Just be thankful you still have
The one good eye you've got.

So don't be bellyachin'
All sad and boo-hoo-hooin'
'Cause you know better than we
That God knows what he's doin'.

****

MANY THANKS, LINE DANCIN' HANK
1991

We've run the gamut
Of dances with you
From Alley Cat
And Gigolo, too.

We've trimmed our
thighs.
We've trimmed our hips,
The world is our oyster,
So now let it rip!

Please accept
Our heartfelt thanks,
You're one fine fella,
LINE DANCIN' Hank!

****

BELATED BEST WISHES FOR YOUR ANNIVERSARY (Bud and Barb Jones)
1991

So sorry that we missed YOUR day---
We're miserable buffoons---
But looking back...
We also missed
Your festive honeymoon.

Guess YOU didn't notice.

HAPPY BIRTHDAY, FAYE (Dawson)
1991

Who is gracious as can be?
Who exudes hospitality?
Who is fine in every way?
It's that gal from Kentucky,
Our good friend, Faye.

Who is perceptive, helpful and kind?
Who is the best friend you'll ever find?
Who enjoys each retirement day?
That gal from Kentucky,
Our good friend, Faye.

Whose talkative nature can engulf a day?
Who goes to lunch and WALKS MILES on
the way?
Whose happy birthday deserves to be
best?

GOOD LORD! IT'S FAYE!
        How did you guess?

****

GET WELL, BETTY KLINGERMAN
1991

When you're "down in the back"
Things are really quite bad
'Cause you're "down in the mouth"
And life is so-o-o sad.

We hear that great pain
Isn't all that you suffer—

Wayne isn't serving
Enough peanut butter!

You do have our sympathy,
Quite seriously given;
We hope you will soon
Be back 'mongst the livin'.

HAPPY BIRTHDAY JOHN CARROLL
1991

One for the money,
Two for the show,
Three to make ready,
Then go, John, go!

Reach for the moon!
Reach for the stars!
You might even touch
Venus and Mars!

But, let's see, now,
How old are you?
Maybe just sitting
On the porch will do.

However you spend it,
Whatever the price,
We hope that your birthday
Will be really nice.

Natalie Biesinger lived down the street from us and most of the women wore shorts all of the time, but Natalie never did. I just couldn't resist writing this poem about her.

NATTY NATALIE (Biesinger)
1991

When Natty Natilie
Works in the yard,
She does it at times
When it seems most
hard.

In the heat of the day!
With the sun bearing
down!

When your eyes go all
squinty
In a puckery frown.

She's out working hard,
Her sweatband in place,
With sunglasses and all,
You can't see her face.

Far be it from me

To make smart retorts,
But I really do like
Natty Natalie's shorts!

Now she is WITH IT!
A true Florida gal!
When she works in the
yard,
She's the cat's meow!

****

My daughter Lisa wanted a poem for her 32nd birthday. I wrote several trying to find one that fit the occasion, but in the end I sent all of them.

HAPPY BIRTHDAY, LISA (32nd)
1991

#1

This is sent along the way
To wish you happiness today.

May all your pleasures be the best,
Your work load light so you can rest.

May all your grades be straight A plus,
And your life continue without fuss.

We hope good wishes apply today
        But if they don't—
HAPPY BIRTHDAY, anyway!

#2

What happens to you
As you attain 32
And you're still
A college coed?

It's the same as before,
Just add one year more,

And your budget
Is still in the red.

Today is Lisa's birthday
I think we'll celebrate—
        She's back in school
        And we're not fools
'Cause SHE is paying the freight.

70

#3

A million kisses,
A thousand hugs,
A ton of good wishes,
Freedom from bugs.

All these fine things
We're wishing for you
'Cause today is your birthday—
BE HAPPY! Please do!

#4
OUR LITTLE GIRL (Daughter Lisa)

Once there was a little girl,
But hey! That's in the past.
Now that girl is all grown up,
She's 32 at last!

But tell us who is counting?
Have things changed all that much?

Although that girl is married,
She still keeps us in touch.

She's once again a coed
Developing her mind;
I bet if we looked deep inside,
That little girl we'd find.

#5

Here's a bright carnation,
Some pretty tulips, too.
To bathe your day in flowers
And send you good luck to you.

We aren't totally senile
So here's a great news flash!
Please find a check somewhere within
Representing good, hard cash.

****

HAPPY BIRTHDAY (Joanna Houghton)
1991

The Fourth of July!
My, what a date!
Recording for posterity
Many things great.

The birth of a nation,
The birth of a child;

Firecrackers bursting,
Celebrations wild.

Anthems and marches
Exuberantly played,
Picnics and gatherings
And stately parades.

Imagine that it all
Was conjured for YOU
And accept our good
wishes
For a HAPPY BIRTHDAY,
too.

****

When my sister's husband, Charles Houston II was hospitalized, Wayne and I went to
Pennsylvania to see him. I sent this card to my sister, Jennivee, when we returned home.

71

THANKS A MILLION
1991

Many thanks for your fine cooking,
The quilt show and the slides;
The trip to Eighty-four
Was a most enjoyable ride.

We wish Charlie a quick recovery
So, perhaps you can visit us;
If you could come in your camper,
It wouldn't be much of a fuss.

TED AND CLAIRE BeWaRE
1991

Welcome to our neighborhood,
We heartily do greet you;
Also so we will tell about
Street rules that may unseat you.

Common sense will tell you
Of which rules you should abide;
But you're in an odd position
And we warn you, don't be snide!

Always greet your neighbors
With a kind word or a nod;
Never park your car
On someone else's sod.

'Cause the *first* time that you skinny dip
In the middle of the night,
We all will come a running
To witness that rare sight!

WELCOME BUD AND BARB (Jones)
1991

A hearty welcome
To Loch Ness;
Hope you'll like
Our street the best.

We're not lofty like a steeple—
We're just
UNCOMMONLY RARE,
OUTSTANDING,
STREET PEOPLE!!!

****

Neighbors Ted and Claire Ware had a swimming pool at their house. Several times they invited the "street people" to come over for an afternoon by the pool. Toni Kartye hosted a thank you party for Ted and Claire. I was asked to write the following poem.

THANK YOU TED AND CLAIRE
1991

For the many hours
Of frolicking in the sun,
For all the sips and snacks we've shared,
The laughter and the fun,

We thank you warmly Ted and Claire,
For all the good you've done.

From the Loch Ness Street People

P.S. And now that we've been proper
And we've done that thank you thing,
Don't you think the time has come
To have another fling?

****

We sent this next thank you to a real estate agent in Hammond, Louisiana when he helped Wayne and I find a place for our daughter, Lori, after she had accepted a position in the Southeastern Louisiana University library. She was to be Head of the Government Documents Department.

OUR THANKS TO YOU
1991

We thank you for your kindness
And for the time you spent
In helping us to find a place
For Lori Lynn to rent.

We think that she will love it
Not just a little, but a bunch;
And if she, too, agrees with us---
She may take you to lunch!

PLAY IT LOUD AND CLEAR (Tim and Lisa Brakel)
1991

Another anniversary?
Is it really your third?
The marriage must have taken "taken"
But GOOD! MY WORD!

There's no turning back now,
You are partners forever

In all that you wish,
In all that you endeavor.

So kick up your heels,
Have a marvelous day,
Celebrate this occasion
In a grandiose way.

THANK YOU FOR THE KEEPING OF THE KEY
1991
(Written for Howard and Joanna Houghton)

Thanks for being the keepers
Of our little Loch Ness place;

You deserve a cooling breeze
Brushing gently 'cross your face.

73

Attach this to your fan,
Resolutely pull the string,

Sit down and have a cool one,
Because you deserve a fling.

* * * *

We took a trip back to Indiana and the following poems were our thanks to some of those we visited.

The first poem was written for Bob and Margie Smith, my husband's brother and his wife. They had five children and one bathroom so they renovated it in a rather unique way. They put in two side by side stools with a partition between and two side by side sinks.

THANKS A MILLION
1991

We thank you for the bedroom
And the cooling of the fan;
And for the use of dual sinks
And the uniquely fashioned "can."

We sang a duet as we did wet,
Then brushed our teeth in time
And there we have the word we seek
To end this 'thank you' rhyme.

P.S.
Sorry we missed Buford
(a China Pig that they had formerly owned)
But we simply couldn't bear it,
Pigs traditionally are FAT
And, unfortunately, we, too, share it!

THANKS FOR THE QUEEN SIZE BED
1991
(Written for Tim and Lisa Brakel)

We thank you for the queen-size bed
And bath amenities,
For the food that you prepared
And for the front door key.

We hope to be forgiven
For refusing Foffie's gift (their cat's hair ball)

But trust that it enhanced your day
And gave that "special" lift.

So sorry that we missed you, Tim,
But doubt that you missed us;
We hope you'll get that contract soon
For a PH D OR BUST!

* * * *

Written for Fran and Tom Casto. Their daughter, who was a flute student, gave a recital as one of our Music Lovers Programs. They had asked me to type her program.

ANOTHER LOAF OF BREAD
1991

I wasn't really begging
For another loaf of bread;
I offered just a thank you
That needed to be said.

Good breeding sometimes shows
In situations such as this;
I always did as mother said,
Not a lesson did I miss.

She said--

"If you are seeking riches
And you must beg for bread,
Never look for just a crumb,
Seek one full loaf instead."

Through you, Fran, we've been repaid
For learning lessons well,
And, golly gee, what can we say?
Except—
YOUR BAKING SURE IS SWELL!

****

This one was written for Katie Jones, who ran a music store at the Lake Square Mall. She came to Scottish Highlands to offer a beginning six-week course on the organ. I bought a $200 dollar organ and joined her class.

THE ORGAN TEACHER
1991

A piece of paper with little black dots
All scattered along in rows;
Other symbols and curlicues—
All Greek to this old schmo.

But as the teacher looks at it
Her eyes light up so grand,
She knows the meanings of all those signs
On the paper she holds in her hand.

She knows how the flow
Of the rhythm should go,
And the sounds to embellish each note;

Will it be soft or loud
Or stately and proud?
She silently ponders her vote.

Then, lo and behold,
As the lesson unfolds
Her grand scheme falls into place

You know she has thought well
And it is clear as a bell;
She performs her music with grace.

We listen enthralled
To the notes, one and all
As the music rolls forth from her hands.

Will we ever be
Half as good as she
Will we ever sound half so grand?

75

I made this next poem into a little booklet and presented it to each of the other eight who lived on our cul-de-sac. Neighbor Jack Pfau cut out of very thin wood tiny little swim trunks which I painted red. I added a black belt with a gold buckle and glued a row of cotton around the bottom of the legs. I attached magnets to the back of Santa's swim trunks which could be stuck on the refrigerator to be used as a note holder.

LOCH NESS CHRISTMAS
1991

T'was the night before Christmas
When out on the street
Everything was silent
And looked really neat.

Ribbons and bows
With lights and what not
Made Loch Ness look better
Than any street of the lot.

There were holly trees and candles
And wreaths flecked with snow,
The people were all sleeping
Dreaming Santa would show.

Sure enough he appeared
In the sky overhead,
But that Florida heat
Was something to dread!

He whisked down quite quickly,
Then hid behind a tree;
He was sweating profusely
And was as wet as could be.

He wrung out his suit,
Then hung it on a bush,
He put on a swimsuit
That barely covered his tush.

At first he felt naked
And hugged himself tight
This new Florida freedom
Filled him with delight.

He was a droll sight
As he stepped here and there,
Then slowly began to prance
And dance with a flair.

He whirled past Ware's pool
In a glorious spin;
He stopped short and stared,
Then belly-flopped in.

Ted and Claire heard the splash
And rushed to look out
To where Santa was floating
With his beard spread about.

Ted got on the phone,
Telling Betty and Jack
To come and see Santa
Swimming out back.

He next called the Smiths
Saying, "Santa's out here,"
Wayne said to Leona,"
"Ted's had too much beer."

He called Joanna and Howard
Saying, "Santa's at play."
They didn't believe him
And crawled back in the hay.

Toni and Don,
Midst the clatter and fuss,
Said, "We want a picture,
Don't forget us!"

76

Natalie and Frank
Were wakened by the lights
That shone on Loch Ness
That Christmas Eve night.

They banged on the door
Of neighbors John and Frona
Who weren't quite awake,
But said they'd bring bologna.

Bud and Barb gathered
Along with the pack
To view a half-naked Santa
Who was miserably stacked!

Though you won't believe it,
So help us, it's true,
They swam and cavorted
And frolicked till 2:00.

Santa bowed politely

And thanking one and all,
He said, "This is the first time
I've had such a ball."

He said, "You don't really
Need any gifts from me,
You already have the best
From what I can see."

The street people waved
As if it were planned,
As he yelled, "MERRY CHRISTMAS
To the whole Loch Ness clan."

"I'll leave you this
Lest this event be debunked,"
He handed each couple
Miniature Santa Claus trunks.

M E R R Y   C H R I S T M A S

****

THANK YOU, HANK AND HILDA
1991

We thoroughly enjoyed your grand party
Presented with such charm and wit;
As I said, "We're just 'clods' from the country,"
But we did have a mighty good sit.

Here's to Hank who, at seventy looks better,
FAR better than anyone should,
May you have a grand year
Filled with great cheer
And enjoy EVERYTHING that is GOOD.

****

John and Frona Carroll gave each couple on Loch Ness Court a gift of an open, ceramic, legal size envelope that stood upright allowing letters to be kept in it. Each one had our own Loch Ness address painted on it. It was also adorned with hand-painted flowers. My husband and I used ours for outgoing mail, which I still do as of this writing, which is September 12, 2015.

THANK YOU JOHN AND FRONA
1991

Letters are great treasures
Bearing bits of news;
How nice to have a receptacle
To keep them in full view.

A glance will spark a memory
Of a written word or two
Causing us to reflect upon
The wish for a fond review.

****

I sent this poem to Tim and Lisa, and also to daughter Lori. It was accompanied by a little wooden outhouse bank which Frank Biesinger had built from a pattern given to him by John Carroll. If I remember correctly, when a coin was dropped into the toilet seat, it tripped a mouse trap and scared the living daylights out of the person who had dropped the coin. I also retitled this poem "Wedding Wishes" later and sent it to a couple who were getting married. It was in my 1991 file but I have forgotten to whom it was sent.

YOUR SAVING GRACE
1991

May sunshine always greet you,
May an outhouse always seat you.
To savor what life has to offer,
May you always have a full coffer.

May your riches be worthwhile and many
And improve when you start saving
pennies.

To receive even more than you've asked,
Start your savings with this.
HAVE A BLAST!

(Please detach the coin from the card and
drop it into your new bank!)

****

TEMPORARILY PERMANENT
1991

"Permanent" would intimate
Continuance forever
Until one gets a "permanent wave"
Then it's simply a word that is clever.

If nomenclature was correct
A lady would say,
"I'm getting a curl at the shop today
That is temporarily permanent."

****

Wayne bought a used bass fishing boat in 1991. I bought a rear view mirror for it. And, of course, a suitable poem had to accompany it.

MAGIC MIRROR ON THE BOAT
1991

Magic mirror on the boat
Tell me, have we crossed a moat?
Perhaps we passed an alligator
Or maybe an old incinerator?
Whatever it is, never fear,
You can view it all
Looking ahead to the rear.

****

In 1991, daughter, Lori, moved from St. Louis, Missouri to Hammond, Louisiana. We gave her a loan to make the move. To even up the score between our two daughters, because if we gave to one daughter we always tried to always give an equal amount to the other, at Christmas we wiped out Lori's debt to us and gave Lisa the same amount in cash. Somehow, Lori could not view her share as a gift. As of this day (9-13-15), I feel she is still resentful. This poem accompanied Lori's gift. (Editor's Note: Not only am I not resentful, I barely remember this event. I am, however, still grateful for the "loan.")

EVENING UP THE SCORE (LORI)
1991

Picture this—a tranquil scene—
With one less debt to pay;

We know you'll be exuberant
On this almost Christmas Day.

As of today, we do declare
You owe us nothing more;

We pray you'll pay yourself instead
To even up the score.

You need to build a cash reserve
To insure you'll never be
A poor lost soul out on the street
Seeking food and charity!

This poem accompanied Lisa's gift:

EVENING UP THE SCORE (LISA)
1991

Picture this—a tranquil scene--
With money in your pockets;
We warn you now, control yourselves.
Keep both eyes in their sockets!

Perhaps this extra bit of cash
Will help with the PH.D.;
Time will tell if you've managed it well;
We'll just have to wait and see.

As of this day we do declare
We've evened up the score;

It might have been a larger sum
If Lori had owed us more!

****

Wayne resisted joining The Loch Ness Monsters' Band then finally gave in. I sent our friends in Indiana this poem to commemorate the occasion.

WAYNE'S OUT OF HAND
December 12, 1991

Dear Bill and Marilynn (Bird),
Since Wayne is now totally inept,
A situation we all must accept,
    I'll drop a few lines
    And write it in rhyme
Even though I'm not terribly adept.

Wayne now is slipping, you see—
Too much proximity to me;
    He begs to go out
    And travel about
While at home he sits waiting for me.

I tell him to come, go along,
He might like the sound of my "my song"
    He says, "Ballet I don't crave,
    I'd rather go to my grave."
So he sits and he waits all day long.

Thus, culture is passing him by,
His well of deep thoughts has run dry;

    He's slipping you see,
    And all because of me,
So shake your head sadly and sigh,
    P-O-O-O-0R guy!

But...

His mind should quickly improve,
At last he fits into the groove;
    He raises all Hell
    Playing his Loch Ness bells,
He's a MONSTER now! That we can prove!

Yes, he now is a member of our band
That's proclaimed as the best in the land;
    He rattles or he shakes
    Causing dishes to break,
There's your proof that he's now out of hand!

****

THANK YOU SUNSHINE CLUB
1991

We thank you, little ladies,
Of the Haines Creek Sunshine Club;
We tried our best to "shine" for you
And hope we didn't flub.

Your many "Sunshine" dishes
Spread a little joy for all;
When it comes to cooking—
You Baptists do stand tall!

HAINES CREEK BAPTIST CHURCH THANKS
1991

We thank you for the fellowship,
The good food and the fun;
We thank you for the kind applause
When the playing was all done.

We always will remember
How FINE you folks all looked;
And we are thanking most especially
The ones who had to cook.

THANK YOU PATHFINDERS
METHODIST PIE
1991

We thank you for the fellowship,
The sharing and the fun;
We thank you for the clapping
When the playing was all done.

But most of all we thank you
For the wondrous Methodist pie

Which brought pure satisfaction
And created heavy sighs.

We'd always heard that Baptists
Could cook the very best
But after tasting yours—
We may have missed our guess.

THANKS FOX RUN
1991

We thank you for the fellowship,
The fine food and the fun,
We thank you for the clapping
When the playing was all done.

We always will remember
The warmness and good cheer

As we met adopted parents
Whose memory we hold dear.

It truly did astound us,
Made us feel invigorated!
To know that—at our age--
New families could be created!

BEST WISHES AMANDA ALTVATER
1991

Best wishes as you graduate,
May good luck follow you;
May only jobs that pay a lot
Become the ones you do.

And, if perchance, you seek to rise
By going on to school,
May you attain what you desire—
And always play it cool.

BEST WISHES JOSHUA JETT
1991

Good luck is sometimes happenstance
You are there when it seeks you out;
More often than not, you make your own
Fond wishes come about.

Decide today the kind of luck
Which you will now attain;
Never forget that YOUR SUCCESS
Depends on YOUR OWN BRAIN!

LISA BRAKEL CELEBRATES Another BIRTHDAY!
1992

Once upon a time
As in a nursery rhyme,
There was a child
That we bounced on our knee;
Now time has passed,
She's no longer a lass—
In fact, she is now 33!

It's hard to believe
The accomplishments achieved
As she teaches
But learns more each day;
This year it seems prudent
For Tim to be a student

As she works hard
To bring home the pay.

Whatever is the case,
We know it's a race
That she runs
With the clock on the wall;
So we'll say our two bits
And then we will "git,"
She won't have to slow
Down at all.

Our very quickest words?
HAPPY 33rd!

CORBYN MUSICALE HEARTILY APPLAUDED
(Written for a Scottish Highlands Music Lovers concert.)
1992

We'd like to thank you, Joyce,
For sharing with us your skill;
Your toe-tapping tunes were exemplary,
They most enjoyably filled the bill.

From Big Ben in London to Latin,
From Hawaii to bird sounds and surf;
It was really quite clear to the audience,

That an organ, for you, is home turf.

You certainly pushed the right buttons
For *When the Saints Go Marching In*;
We know you'll be "in that number"
Strolling sedately
To the sounds of Big Ben!

WHAT AN ANGEL YOU ARE, LOUIS
1992

We'd like to thank you, Louis,
For sharing in Joyce's day
By recording for posterity
The marvelous program she played.

We know she will always remember
What a thoughtful neighbor you were
Just as you will always treasure
Your musical memories of her.

(Louis videotaped Joyce Corbyn's performance for Music Lovers Club.)

****

FRIENDS...UNDERSTAND
BELATED HAPPY BIRTHDAY, NAT
1992

We're a little bit late
We must admit
But the older we are,
The later we "git."

Do overlook
Our slip-up, my dear,
And accept this fond wish
For the one next year.

SONSHINERS SCORE A HIT
1992

We most sincerely
Wish to express
Our deepest gratitude.

Your upbeat tunes
Were excellent,
Your vocalist outshone the best;

Your concert was delightful;
One of the best
That we have viewed.

How very fortunate
We all were
To have you as our guests.

THANK YOU WAYNE AND BETTY (Klingerman)
1992

The food was great,
The conversation good.
The evening progressed
Along as it should.

We thank you profusely
For the whole shebang;
'Tis rumored that we ate
Better than we sang.

HAPPY BIRTHDAY, RANDALL
1992

We heard you had a birthday
And couldn't believe our ears;
We heard that you'd been having them
For, lo, these many years.

Three-quarters of a century!
Just think of the birthday cake!

It's a wonder there is any left
For someone else to bake!

Just think of all the frosting
And that gooey birthday stuff;
You'd better start having birthday pies
And leave some cakes for us!

BETTY PFAU HAS A BIRTHDAY
1992

Unless I'm wrong
I do believe
About your birth date
You'd deceive.

But, nevertheless,
I, too, believe,
One card from me
You should receive.

Happy birthday!
Alack and forsooth.
Have I discovered
Your birthday truth?

Well, if it isn't
Close to this date,

You'll have one
sometime;
Good wishes can wait.

And if this verse
Seems awfully long,
I'm covering tracks
In case I'm wrong!

****

My sister, Elva (Heramb) Hayworth, who was ten years my senior, wrote this poem for me.

Hi!
How is Coddie (my family nickname)
That good waddy
Something from newspaper
A real family shaker
This little pup (a picture of a pup was on the paper with the poem)
Would tear things up
I've had my say
About the way
Heramb money should go
A memorial at Farmers Chapel
For one who did not go slow
Then I ate an apple.

I sent the following reply:

LETTER TO ELVA
1992

My dearest sister, Tatie, (her family
nickname)
So long have you repined,
Poetic genius lies dormant—
Because you wouldn't let it shine.

Now that I know your secret,
I'll expect new stanzas from you;
If you'll only keep on writing
Who knows the wonders you'll do?

I have often penned poems to our
children
Relating a trip that we took,
Or wishing another happy birthday
Or reporting that an earthquake had
shook.

I've written of babies and showers
And weddings, anniversaries, and sich;
I've written enough to fill volumes—
Or to give one a mighty big itch.

No literary laurels besieged me,
No prizes ever came my way;
But when poetic license o'ertook me,
By golly, I did have a great day.

Now, let's get back to your poem,
Chocked full of poetic seeds—
If your stanzas are not well accepted,
You can, at least, sprout a few trees!
　　　(You know, the seeds from the
　　　　apple you ate.)

****

HAWTHORNE ENSEMBLE THANK YOU
1992

We thank you most sincerely
From the bottoms of our hearts;
Your program was delightful—
Each and every part.

Those of us who braved the storm,
As music lovers true,
Assign an A plus rating
To every one of you!

REINHARDT THANK YOU
1992

Your concert was delightful,
A potpourri of sound,
On one of the neatest instruments
That we have seen around.

We wish you lots of sales and such
In figures BIG AND BOLD
And hope that you'll recover soon
From that troublesome old cold.

PENNY SCHMITZ SCORES A HIT
Just One Penny
1992

We thank you most sincerely
From the bottoms of our hearts;
Your program was delightful,
Each and every part.

Through you the gods have given us
The ultimate in pleasure—
JUST ONE PENNY!
But, my! What a treasure!

****

One day at Scottish Highlands, a neighbor jokingly asked me if I would be her sister which spawned the following reply.

AUNT CLEOME MAE THANK YOU
1992

As a sister
I will welcome you,
And also as a friend,
But the giving of
Such lavish gifts
Must come to a sudden end. (She had
given me some china.)
For all I
Have to offer back
Is a few well-chosen words,

And Heaven knows
The words I have
Are strictly for the birds.

However, I
Was duly touched
And mighty thankful, too,
That "fate"
Brought us to Loch Ness Court
To share our lives with YOU.

****

I had written a thank you to a performer from Tune Town at the Lake Square Mall for the That's Entertainment group and I had mistaken his name for another. I sent this to the real performer to excuse my error.

KEN WAHLE, IS HIS NAME-O
1992

We send a second thank you
To Ken Wahle—if it really is his name—
Who can attribute my gross error
To one slightly addled dame.

HAPPY BIRTHDAY TO AN OLD MAN (Mr. Ashbaugh)
1992

What can be said to an old man
When he reaches 93?
What advice can be given
When it comes from the likes of me?

Of one thing I am certain
God must love you a lot,
For he gave you an able body
To get to the places you've got.

He endowed you with all of your senses,
With wisdom and virtue and such,

So a cheerful Happy Birthday
From me just doesn't mean much.

But, nevertheless, we wish you
Happiness and good times galore
And hope that the BEST is still coming
NEXT YEAR—YOUR YEAR 94!

> Your pew pals, (He always sat next
> to us at church)
> Wayne and Leona Smith

****

The following poem was my entry in the "WORST RHYMED POEM" contest in 1992. The first line had to be "It was a dark and stormy night..."

HEAD OVER HEELS IN LOVE
1992

It was a dark and stormy night,
Heathcliff and Millicent were lovers in flight.

Said Milly to Cliff as he peered up at the sash,
"Be careful, the lightning might turn you to ash."

He answered, "My darling, come let us flee.
I will battle the elements, yea, the whole world for thee.

So great is my love, for you I would die,
I would mop all the rain from out of the sky."

"That isn't just raindrops you're feeling, my dear,

Your big ladder leans on my fingers right here.
Teardrops do fall from my fluttering eyes.
I can't even think of a romantic sky.

You've mashed them to smithereens and I cannot flee
For I am in pain from my hands to my knees."

Cliff was abashed that so badly he'd erred
And kissed her quite tenderly to show that he cared.

He freed her caressingly, gathered her in his arms;
She clung to him limply, admiring his charms.

87

Loud thunder did boom and lightning did flash
Striking Cliff in a place that he groped unabashed.

He frantically tried to assuage his great pain
But flipped over backward right into the rain.

Milly went, too, in an arc o'er Cliff's head,
And hung bottoms up in a tree by the shed.

Cliff mourned his performance on this happiest of days
And tried desperately to retrieve her, but lacked any way.

Just as he pondered his most woeful state,
Milly tumbled down like a clattering crate.

He reached out to grab her but caught only her hair,
She whizzed right on by but her hair was still there.

Milly landed squarely on the top of her head.
Her neck snapped like a twig and Cliff knew she was dead.

Cliff oft reminisced about the loss of his love,
And wondered what else she had left up above.

****

This was written to Mr. Pringle, the developer of Scottish Highlands.

DEAR MR. PRINGLE
1992

Dear Mr. Pringle,
May we suggest
A kindness from you
To eliminate a mess?

The mess that we speak of
Is really not intended
But one that could reasonably
Quite easily be ended.

The lot next to ours
Is "empty" but, alas,
It's overgrown with weeds;
It's a jungle-like mass.

If you would but level it,
And remove the debris,
My husband has promised
To mow it, you see.

Since Petersons who own it
Won't build for a year;
That year would be better
If our plea you would hear.

Our neighbors would love it,
Our street would look better,
So, please Mr. Pringle,
Consider this letter.

This was for neighbor, John Carroll, who had had surgery.

WISHING YOU A SPEEDY RECOVERY
1992

You're sore,	Could be worse,	We hope
And more.	BIG HEARSE.	You'll cope,
Too bad,	Must confess,	We contend
So sad.	You're blessed.	You'll mend.

IT'S A MATTER OF SEMANTICS (For John and Frona Carroll)
1992

It's a matter of semantics
Each time we hear new words,
Our minds reach out to grasp them
To interpret what we've heard.

Take these two words and use them
(the two words are bestest and monsters)
In whatever way you wish,
Can you see the jocularity of this?
If not—we're both dead fish!

THE BESTEST MONSTERS (For John and Frona Carroll)
1992

In spite of all the laughter,
The joking and the fun;
We hope this anniversary
Will be your happiest one.

We hold you both in high esteem.
You're the finest in the land
For you're the bestest monsters
In the Loch Ness Monsters' band.

John and Frona Carroll

89

This was written for John and Frona Carroll's 10th anniversary.

THE LANGUAGE OF LUV
1992

Seven sinister ministers
Bowed their heads to pray,
One conniv'n' south'en gal
Suggested what they'd say.

Please pray fer Jonn to ax me
To be his luvin' bride,
Ah jest cain't live without him!
Ah MUST walk bah his side.

Although he does say "pa'k the cah"
And tells others ah am Froner,

Deah Lawd, don't let him pass me bah,
'Twould be a dreadful boner!

You know that ah say "ain't" and "cain't"
And also "rahz and shahn"
It ain't how ah say the words that counts
When fer John's luv ah pine.

Please listen to these preacher men
Who pray to God above,
Fer we're speakin' the selfsame language
When we speak the LANGUAGE of LUV.

****

HAPPY ANNIVERSARY TIM AND LISA
1992

Consider your past year,
The activities therein,
You'll see each day jammed full!
You just can't help but grin.

Another hectic year
Is what lies just ahead;
So tackle it with relish,
To assuage lamented dread.

You certainly are DOERS
You make our poor heads spin;
With your noses to the grindstone,
New jobs we know you'll win.

HAPPY ANNIVERSARY!
And as couples often do,
Have a very special meal
For just the two of you.

****

THINKING OF YOU, TONI
1992

Our thoughts are with you, Toni,
As once more we depart,
We'll keep you ever in our thoughts
And always in our hearts.

Do what the doctors order,
We'll trust that they know best;
Do eat all your veggies,
And get a lot of rest.

We'll be calling for reports
Of progress you have made

And hope that your recovery
Will earn an A+ grade.

WE WISH YOU WELL (Agnes Parsons)
1992

So…
You "swallowed" a camera?
Well, glory be!
Glad it was you instead of me!

But also happy to hear you're fine.
Guess a stitch in time
Really does save nine.

GO, TONI, GO!
1992

Rah, rah,
Rah-rah-rah!
Now hear this
One and all!

Peach seeds, biscuits,
All that jazz,
We don't want
No razzamatazz!

We want Toni
To be well;
Buckle down, kid,
And try like _ _ _ _!

HIT THE BOOKS, STUDY HARD (Tim Brakel)
1992

Happy birthday once again
We send our best to you
And hope that you are doing well
In all you strive to do.

And even more, we wish for you,
Your doctorate degree

So we can say to friend or foe
So very naturally,

"Our son-in-law, THE DOCTOR,
Is doing this or that."
We think that it would liven up
The trivialest of chats!

HAVE A HAPPY 30th, LORI
1992

So now you have reached it,
The big three-oh;
Watcha gonna do?
We'd sure like to know.

Will you go in for dancing?
Like, maybe ballet?

Or move out to the country
And start raising hay?

Or will you let life
Flow on as it does,
Usually a hum
With an occasional buzz?

Or will you come up with
A fantastical scheme
That will lead you to realize
Your wildest of dreams?

Well, whatever you do,
We'll still think you're grand
Cause you're our BEST Lori,
THE BESTEST WHAT AM!

****

Written for Frona Carroll after she had surgery. I took her a chocolate pie.

JUST WHAT THE DOCTOR ORDERED
1992

The best thing for a bellyache
May be a soothing balm,
Or maybe it's a little pill
To keep you cool and calm.

But...
Whenever we are hurting,
We two unslender Smiths,
We always try a piece of pie
Quite similar to this.

****

This poem was for my husband's niece, Martha Smith, when she had decided to drop out of Indiana University due to her mother's illness.

PAINT YOURSELF A BRIGHT FUTURE
1992

Never say never
And never let "die"
This attempt you have made—
This gigantic TRY!

Think of the FEES
You'll lose if you quit!

Think of the moss
That will grow if you SIT!

Think of your future
And reach for the sky
We KNOW you can do it!
Hang in there and TRY!

****

Written for John Johnson on the birth of his daughter, Kaylee. John was a teacher at the Oxford, IN school where my husband, Wayne Smith was the principal and I taught third grade.

CONGRATULATIONS ON THE NEW ADDITION
1992

Congratulations by the ton
Are sent to you
For the little one.

But, my, how lonesome
She will be,

This wee small child,
This babe, Kaylee.

Just to even up the score
You need to plan
For at least one more.

WEILENMANN SCORES A SUCCESS
1992

From show tunes to country,
Then on to ragtime and such,
For all of your effort
We thank you so much.

We laud your fine talent,
Applauding the fact
That you allowed us
To share your great act.

PEN PALS SCORE A SUCCESS!
1992

From show tunes to country,
Then on to Cohan and such,
For all of your effort we thank you,
We thank you and thank you so much.

We laud your fine talent,
Applauding the fact
That you allowed us
To share your great act.

BELLRINGERS SCORE A SUCCESS!
1992

We'd like to thank you kindly
For appearing here today;
What a pleasure it has been
To come and hear you play.

Your talents are magnificent
Your music was the best
How fortunate we were
To have you as our guests.

SCOTTISH HIGHLANDS OFFERS THANKS
1992

Pianos stand for many things
Within the scope of living
But, in your case, yours became a gift
That you gave through the love of giving.

And so we now send back to you
Our very hearty thanks!
When we consider all the saints,
You're assured a topmost rank.

MIXED CHORUS SCORES A SUCCESS
1992

Christmas is quite special
Because of many things;
One of the very best,
Is hearing a chorus sing.

We laud your fine talent
Applauding the fact
That you allowed us
To share your great act.

THANK YOU CAROL ADAMS
1992

Elegantly she dances
So daintily each step,
Hopefully she strives
To make us all adept.

But, in her heart of hearts,
That *Achy Breaky* one,
She knows we all have two left feet!

She teaches just for fun?

So-------------

Thank you for the fellowship,
Thank you for the fun,
Thanks for all the teaching
That so patiently you have done.

****

I wrote the following poem and sent it in to a newspaper columnist –I can't remember which one but he wrote for *The Orlando Sentinel*. He had written a column extolling the virtues of boiled peanuts.

HEY, WE TRIED 'EM
1992

We stopped and tried boiled peanuts,
'Twas good we saw a sign,
For the fellow who was selling them
Was busy all the time.

We asked, "How do you fix them?"
He replied, "We 'bawl' them, son,
When they is all 'bawled'
We know that they be done."

The samples that he offered
Were still a wee bit damp,

Those poor wet, soggy peanuts,
Those hot "bawled" little scamps

We cracked open steaming shells,
Popped the morsels in our mouths
It took one chomp to mash them,
Then we promptly spat them out.

They tasted like potatoes,
A flat, unsavory kind—
It's no wonder those "bawled" peanuts
Just puddled up and whined.

At Scottish Highlands money had been raised to buy an organ for the auditorium. I wrote the following thank you to the residents as a representative of the That's Entertainment Committee, which was the new name for the Music Lovers Club.

Betty Klingerman, who had been the founder of the Music Lovers Club, was much maligned by many of the residents because they felt she was pushing her own personal agenda by requesting a new organ. Betty, of course, was thinking only of the pleasure that such an organ could bring to Scottish Highlands' residents through community concerts. Betty deserved better treatment. In fact, the community, as a whole, owed her a great deal because she was a fine musician who performed at any and every function where her talents could be used.

THE ORGAN IS AN ASSET TO OUR COMMUNITY
1992

Thank you! Thank you! THANK YOU!   We'll do our best to entertain.
From the bottoms of our hearts.   And hope we'll do enough
Our committee has been granted   To show that Scottish Highlanders
One spanking brand new start.   Are made of strutting stuff!

The That's Entertainment committee composed of myself, Natalie Biesinger, Barbara Jones, and Betty Pfau presented the new organ at a concert in May of 1992. I had made a banner and wrote the following words to commemorate the occasion.

Each person who came to the concert received a blown-up balloon on a string and a straight pin which we pinned to their collars or lapels. They were told to wait for further instructions.

DEDICATION CEREMONY

(Unroll the banner slowly.)

First committee member: (Holds one end of the banner.)

No matter what you're feeling
No matter how much fuss,
The organ now is paid for,
Please celebrate with us.

Second committee member: (Unrolls her end of the banner.)

Let's put it all behind us
I'm sure you'll get the hang,
Let's shatter all illusions
With one big, solid bang!

Third committee member: (Demonstrates holding a balloon in one hand a pin in the other.)

Kindly take your pin
Also your balloon
Turn down all the hearing aids
Lest one should faint or swoon.

Fourth committee member: (Group pops balloon as she demonstrates.)

Thanks to the Community Council
It's all been settled now
When I give the word, just do it,
POP your balloon—KAPOW!

****

MANY HAPPY RETURNS (Lisa)
1993

No sentimental tribute,
No syrupy sweet stuff,
Just knowing you're OUR daughter
Is virtually enough!

So HAPPY BIRTHDAY once again
'Tis older that you be;

If you keep getting older
You'll soon be as old as we!

And then you'll know the truth of it,
What we have known for years;
Each day as you grow older,
You also grow more dear.

****

After we moved to Florida, I served on the committee to plan an annual luncheon meeting for the Indiana State Teachers Association-Retired (ISTA-Retired) members who lived in the central Florida area. The Loch Ness Monsters that Wayne and I played with had been asked to perform at the luncheon. The speaker was to be the director of ISTA-Retired. His name was Dale Harris. I wrote the following words to be sung to the tune of *Buford* by Randall and Agnes Parsons.

My sister, Elva, had passed away in Indiana so Wayne and I were not able to attend the luncheon but we were told that the song went over quite well.

DALE HARRIS 'N' STUFF
1993

Dale Harris went into the city
Ped-dl-ling changes—'n' STUFF
He tried to influence lawmakers
To fool them and then call their bluff.

CHORUS;
Dale has become a great hero
He's championed our causes—'n' STUFF
Now we receive 13 payments
But, Dale, we say that AIN'T enough.

We all have taught many lessons,
Readin' 'n' writin'—'n' STUFF
We think you should try for a 14th
So retirement won't be quite so tough.

CHORUS:

Don't ever be kind to lawmakers
Their "pore" heads are all filled with—
STUFF
If they won't meet our requirements,
You may have to get pretty rough.

Tomorrow when you're in the Senate,
Representing teachers—'n' STUFF
You must be strict with those lawmakers
Show them that you can get gruff.

CHORUS:
Don't tippy toe through the tulips,
Just SLAP them alongside the head
Don't say we advised you to do it
Cause we can't AFFORD to be dead!

****

In Florida we have love bugs, so called because they die after mating, but the worst part about them is that you never see just one—always two—and they are stuck together mating! They appear once in the spring and again in the fall. I wrote this as a contest entry for the *Orlando Sentinel*. I didn't win the contest. (Sing to the tune of *I Love You Truly*.)

I LOVE YOU LOVE BUGS
1993

I love you love bugs,
Truly do,
Life would be pleasant
Without you.

Your disgusting "hang-ups"
Are strange to see.
I'm glad it affects *you*
And not me!

****

Dr. Spivey operated on my right, middle finger.

TRIBUTE TO DR. SPIVEY
1993

Here is a tribute to Spivey,
Doctor Extraordinaire, indeed!
He rose to the challenge when asked to
And fulfilled my unusual need.

My *bad finger* sports a new joint now,
More useful than I'd hoped to expect.
I display it in public with pride
And guess what?
Viewers don't even get upset!

****

Sonya Yates was my occupational therapist for my finger surgery.

THANKS TO SONYA YATES
1993

As to the health of my finger,
To this I can fully attest,
The OT at Jewett named Sonya
Is truly the absolute best.

Now, to my friends' consternation,
Metamorphosis has surely occurred;
My big joint has shrunken to average;
It must have been MAGIC! My Word!

****

The *Los Angeles Daily News* requested that anyone who had enjoyed Jimmy Stewart's movies send him a birthday card. I, of course, had to do my own thing.

TRIBUTE TO JIMMY STEWART
1993

What can one say to an old man
When he reaches year 85?
W'al, I'll tell ya one thing,
He's darned lucky to still be alive!

And if he is named Jimmy Stewart,
Stalwart champion of the screen,

He deserves accolades beyond number—
He's fulfilled an American dream.

He's become a renowned institution,
Applauded in all movie halls,
So do have a GRAND HAPPY BIRTHDAY
And, w'al, Jimmy, I guess that's all.

BETH GRADUATES
1993

Our heartiest congratulations
Are sent along the way
To wish for you the happiest
Of graduation days!

You may think you are finished
With books and all that stuff,

But, better keep on pluggin'
Cause you can't *ever* learn enough.

May you make the wisest choices
In everything you do
And make your parents proud
That they created you!

JON WEDDLE GRADUATES
1993

Our heartiest congratulations
Are sent along the way
To wish for you the happiest
Of graduation days.

May luck be ever with you,
Good fortune by your side;

May you always make wise choices
With ambition as your guide.

And just to prove we're useful
We'll help you get a start
Please accept this token offering—
Now, hey! We've done our part!

CONGRATULATIONS LORI AND MICHAEL
1993

Congratulations to you both
On this your wedding day;
May all the things you wish for
Also come your way.

May love be ever in your hearts
And bliss shine in your eyes—
Aw, shucks. Let's don't get maudlin'!
Just have a good life, you guys!

HAPPY BIRTHDAY, TIMOTHY
1993

Here's to you on your birthday!
An auspicious occasion indeed,
With fatherhood looming before you
Good wishes aren't all that you need.

So here is some fast cash to fritter,
For one grand fling, if you please;
As usual, you'll notice and wonder
How spending can be such a breeze.

HOPE YOUR DAY IS A BLAST
Tim and Lisa's First Anniversary
1993

"Happy Anniversary!" most folks say,
To wish you bliss for one short day;
But we have wishes grandiose,
We want each day to be the most;
And when you've racked up one whole year,
We'll send more greetings, little dears.

MOM'S MUSINGS ON A VERY NOTEWORTHY OCCASION
1993
(For daughter Lori Smith)

Happy Birthday! Happy Birthday!
A repetitive loud shout;
Some ladies in their 30s
Might want to kick well-wishers out.

Perhaps it would be better
To remove a year instead

Each year you would get younger
Your age would never move ahead.

Longevity, however,
Might leave you all forlorn;
You might end your life much younger
Than you were when you were born!

HAPPY BIRTHDAY, PETE
September 20, 1993

One year more than the one before,
They just keep racking up;
You are no longer spritely and agile
Or running around like a pup.

But consider your age and your wisdom,
Of both you have quite enough
To those who revel around you--

You can still pull off a good bluff.

Pretending can be therapeutic
In making you feel younger still;
So think STRONG, AGILE, and YOUTHFUL,
It might pep you up like a pill.

HAPPY BIRTHDAY, THELMA MOYARS
1993

No eternal words of wisdom
Or cleverly worded advice;
We'll just wish a grand Happy Birthday
To someone especially nice!

No hat to flip off with a flourish,
No bowing or scraping and such,
We'll offer a sincere Happy Birthday
To one we revere very much!

MERRY CHRISTMAS, CAROL
(Carol Adams, Line Dance Teacher)
1993

Western jeans of faded blue,
Straps with buckles on your shoes,
Square-cut toes that dip and dive,
Hip swingin'! Heel stompin'!
      MAN ALIVE!

Yes, western dance is now your style
These new routines induce a smile;

Perhaps, in time, we'll learn them, too.
But never quite as well as you.

Through it all we love you dearly
And kindly thank you most sincerely;
Merry Christmas, li'l "podner," gal,
From all your western dancin' pals.

****

My husband had written a poem for his sister, Joyce. She mistakenly sent a thank you to me because I was usually the one who wrote the poems. This was my reply to her.

Dear Joyce,
Credit is great when credit is due
But I didn't write that poem for you;
I only typed it to make it look neat
And, in truth, it was penned by—
Your own brother, Pete!!!

****

Somehow our two daughters arranged a surprise 40th Wedding Anniversary party. They invited all of The Loch Ness Monsters. Our daughter, Lori, had already arrived from her home in St. Louis, Missouri for Christmas so she got everything ready for the party while their dad and I drove to Orlando Airport to pick up daughter Lisa and her husband, Tim. I sent the following poem to each family that had attended.

WE DIDN'T "CARROT" ALL THAT YOU SCORED A HIT
1993

We'd like to thank you one and all
For sharing in "our day,"
You've made it much more meaningful
In each and every way.

Never more shall we assume
That we're in charge of our domain
But, if it means a party,

We'll step aside and not complain.

HOWEVER!!!! HENCEFORTH------

When we speak, eye to eye
With a-n-y o-n-e o-f y-o-u
We'll wonder if the words you say
Really might be true!

We'll cherish all the memories
Created by y'all

And, hey, you really got us, guys,
You should be standing **tall**.

****

In the spring of 1993 our daughter, Lisa, asked if I would type up instructions for the main canning and freezing methods that I had used through the years to preserve produce from my husband Wayne's garden. Wayne was better known as Pete by family and friends. As usual, I seem to think in rhyme as a first form of expression so, for my Home Preservation Cookbook, I created this motto:

To preserve your home,
Feed your man;
Stuff it in a Ziploc
Or dump it in a can.

Then to honor the title "Ziploc Queen" which daughters Lisa and Lori had bestowed on me, I felt it was necessary to pay homage to the mighty Ziploc.

Ziplocs here, Ziplocs there
We use Ziplocs without care—
Stuff 'em full of piecrust
Stuff 'em full of corn
So we can stuff ourselves
Like we have since we were born!

Then I divided the foods I preserved into groups:

CRUNCHIN' BUNCH

Crunch 'em in a colander,
Squeeze 'em down tight;
When the insides are out,
You've done 'em up right.
(Applesauce, grape juice, plum butter, tomato juice.)

POD GODS

Pick 'em off a bush
Pop 'em out in your hand,
They're a match made in Heaven
And they surely look grand.
(Peas lima beans, green beans.)

102

THE 'ERRY ONES

The 'erry' ones are best
When baked in a pie
And someone is breathin'
A satisfied sigh.
(Blackberries, cherries, gooseberries.)

****

I thought it would be fun during our retirement to write to manufacturers with my comments about their products. I sent the following one to Myers Packing Company of Temple, Pennsylvania.

DEAR SIRS (MUSHROOMS)
1994

Pennsylvania Dutchman, our mushroom of choice,
Is usually a treat for which we rejoice;
BUT—our most recent purchase was woefully lacking
When out popped this *grass* from the watery packing.
We are not perfect but we wanted you to know
Your inspector was asleep or dreadfully slow!

During the same period, Charmin came out with their big rolls of Ultra toilet tissue. I wrote what I thought of it, but didn't have the nerve to actually mail the poem to them.

DEAR SIRS (TOILET TISSUE)
1994

For years I've bought Charmin,
It has served us well.
But your big rolls of Ultra?
There's a sad tale to tell.

The sheets are too soft,
Therein lies the rub

For it balls up and stays *there*,
Then is shed in the tub.

I do like your products,
We've used them for years
But, alas, your good Charmin
Now stands in arrears!

103

WE WERE AS PROUD AS A PEACOCK (For Penny Schmitz--Pianist)
At an Indiana Retired Teachers Luncheon
At Vic's Embers in Leesburg, Florida
1994

We'd like to thank you Penny,
For your entertaining way,
Your zippy tunes and rhythms
Made us wish that we could play.

There were very few among us
Who failed to tap or grin—

Just remember that we were all teachers
When pleasure was a sin.

Most, of course did love you,
And related to your style,
Especially when they witnessed
The sunny brightness of your smile.

PARSONS DOWN BUT NOT OUT!
(For Randall Parsons after eye surgery; 9-12-94)

Feeling momentarily
Considerably quite warily
Just a l-it-tle bit "contrarily?"

Gr-r-r-it your teeth and hang on tight,
Suffer through it

And you'll be alright.

We'll commiserate along the way
And pray you'll improve
Each and every day.

THE NUMBERS GAME
(For Lisa Brakel; 1-12-94)

Once we had a daughter,
We ranked her as a ten,
But, when she was with child
We had to think again.

Although each happy birthday
Is better than the last,

We don't know what to say
Since she's become a one and a half!

I guess we'll just stick with it,
The same old tried and true--
Have a happy birthday, Lisa
All one and a half of you!

WE HOPE YOU HAVE A BALL
(For Mrs. Toop's Birthday; 1-28-94)

If we could be wee tiny elves
Tucked away upon a shelf,
We'd tip our hats and bow to you,
Then say, "HELLO AND HOW-DEE-DO?"

While we were there
We'd wish you well—
Have a GRAND HAPPY BIRTHDAY
Good friend, Elma Belle!

ON THE OCCASION OF PARENTHOOD
(For Tim and Lisa Brakel; March 31, 1994)

Another day is dawning—
The two of you are now three,
No need to mop or sweep now
The floors that you can't see.

No time is left for wondering
What you'd do with free time to spend;
No need to buy postage for letters,
There's no time to write them or send.

The REAL pleasures of life await you
As you watch this new baby grow,
Each antic or phase will be cuter
Than anyone else's you know.

So cherish your role now as parents;
You've experienced the gamut of bliss,
Just one thing more will be better—
When you add one sibling to this!

ADVICE FROM YOUR GRANDPARENTS TO YOU!
(For Wayne P. Brakel; March 31, 1994)

Consider yourself a lucky child,
One who is blessed, indeed.
You have two parents who love you,
To provide whatever you need.

Consider us, too, while you're thinking,
Know who we are, goodness sakes!
We're the parents of your mom,
We're the icing on your little cake!

****

For Reverend Bill Fraker of the First United Methodist Church of Tavares, Florida. I worked a half day a week in his office for two years.

HERE'S THE SCORE! BILL IS 59!
1994

What advice can one give to a parson
When he reaches a ripe 59?
It's better to enjoy than to abhor it
'Cause 60 is just down the line.

When one contemplates future decades,
The 70s, the 80s, and all,
Fifty-nine ain't too bad to be bein'—
It may be your best year of all.

┿┿┿┿

For Kurt and Maureen Schultze who moved to Texas from Oxford, Indiana. They had been faithful members of our church and if I remember correctly, I was asked to write this for them to celebrate their retirement.

105

CHANGES
1994

Once upon a time many years ago
I was asked to write a poem—
Why me? I didn't know.

You, Maureen, would copy it
In fine calligraphy
And present it to Dan Motto, (our
minister at that time)
For all the church to see.

In the final desperate moments
Before the presentation
I penned that heartfelt thank you
On behalf of the congregation.

All of this came at Christmastime
When I was rushed indeed,
I composed the words in utter haste
And delivered them with speed.

Late that night as I tossed and turned,

Those words kept coming back
And as they tumbled through my mind,
I knew the "train had missed the track."

Before I hustled off to school
When day had dawned at last,
I called you up to CHANGE some words,
But your part was done. It was past!

All of these years it has haunted me,
That echo from the past,
Did you leave the words I told you first?
Or, did you CHANGE them right at the
last?

At any rate, whatever the case,
Wayne and I send to you our best;
Oxford has been graced by your
presence,
The community has truly been blessed.

****

AGNES PARSONS, IT'S YOUR DAY!
(For Agnes Parsons on her 70th birthday; 11-20-94.)

Birthdays come, birthdays go,
Some add wrinkles,
Some don't show.
Most we'd rather do without,
So why not turn them round about?

Instead of always ADDING years.
Take some away!
'Twill bring on cheers.

Be careful how you do your math
Or it could be a dang'rous path!

About you, dear, it might be said,
"Her age is running in the red!"
They'd blow their whistles
And toot their horns
Saying, "She's younger now
Than when she was born!"

****

In October of 1994, Wayne and I were advised by his heart doctor to go on a cruise… or
something….to celebrate his successful five bypass heart surgery in April of that year. We

had also reached our fortieth year of marriage in December in 1993, so we viewed this trip as a celebration of that milestone as well. We booked passage on the Holland Line's Nieuw Amsterdam for a tour of the western Caribbean. I wrote the following account of this very memorable trip.

FORTY YEARS AT SEA
1994

This saga of the sea
For just Pete (Wayne) and me
Began a long time ago;
We schemed and we dreamed
But it never really seemed
That in real life we'd ever get to go.

Our fortieth wedding date came
We were both somewhat lame
Fate lopped us down with one arm;
I had a dizzy streak
And Pete's heart was weak—
But we both recovered without too much harm.

In the summer of '94
To settle the score
We charted a Caribbean cruise;
We paid two thousand three,
Headed on out to sea.
Said goodbye to those landlubber blues.

My birthday arrived (Oct. 15th)
We buzzed 'round the hive
Packing our last dab of clothes;
If any suitcase burst
Mine would be first,
They were almost too full to close.

We'd scrubbed the house clean
And worked like machines,
We gathered our passports 'n' stuff.
Taking one look around
Out the door we bound,
Of preparations, we'd had quite enough!

We gassed up the car
But didn't go far,
Our minds seemed to be all afloat;
The air was quite cool
And I was no fool,
We returned home to get one more coat.

We were soon on our way
With light traffic that day.
We stopped for our last meal on land;
The Cracker Barrel was great
Though we did have to wait
At Tampa where we made our last stand.

We arrived at the ship,
Impressively equipped—
Much grander and bigger than we thought;
We waited and waited
Until we were sated
With sitting much longer than we ought.

As three p.m. came
We were ready to blame
Everyone for this lengthy delay;
But boarding began
According to plan,
Up the gangplank we soon made our way.

We were greeted sincerely,
Led to our stateroom quite cheerily,
Our bags were waiting for us;
We took a quick look around
Till everything we'd found,
Unpacked and stowed away without fuss.

At four p.m. we trekked
To the Upper Promenade Desk
And were given lifeboat instructions;
Our jackets had to be tight
And laced up just right,
Our lives might depend on this induction.

At five, we watched from the deck,
As the ship started its trek
Away from its berth by the pier;
The motors rumbled and quaked,
The ship left quite a wake,
As the people on deck loudly cheered.

We bathed and then dressed
So we'd look our best
In our elegantly casual wear;
A travel talk on ports
Was pointedly short
As we moved to the dining room there.

Six hundred were seated,
New table mates greeted,
A flutter of napkins fanned the air;
Richard, our waiter,
Quite ably did cater
To all of our needs, pair by pair.

There were so many utensils
I needed a pencil
To remember the usage for each;
Nine pieces in all,
Big kinds and small
But all were within easy reach.

The napkins were folded
As if they were molded
Into a neat shape every night;
If I waited a while
Richard would smile
And place mine just perfectly right.
The Northcutts were there
Looking quite debonair
Exclaiming over this and o'er that,

The Edelsteins were in place,
We sat face to face
And in no time we started to chat.

Bill Clifford chimed in
With his know-it-all grin,
He inspected casinos at sea;
His banter was clever
As he did endeavor
To enlighten us all—even me!

He had been everywhere,
Done everything there,
Fascinating us all with his charm;
For any question we had
He was more than just glad.
To inform us to keep us from harm.

The seven course dinner
Left me a bit thinner
But the others exclaimed with delight;
Each course seemed finer
To all gourmet diners
But, for me, it was a very long night!

Entertainment ensued
And we practically cooed,
The orchestra really was grand;
Dan Van Palta played,
This banjo strummer swayed,
He commanded an ear-splitting hand.

The dancers were curvaceous
And more than courageous
As they sang and they pranced 'round the
floor;
But soon it all ended
And we slowly wended
Our way through the crowds at the door.

On Sunday we awoke
But hardly even spoke
As we sleepily look for the Lido,
We needed coffee and tea

To awaken such as we,
Were we searching a haystack for a
needle?

The Lido became
Our place between games,
Where we had all our breakfasts and
lunches;
I can honestly say
Many did it our way,
We were always among hordes and
bunches.

To a tour talk we went
Because we were bent
On learning all we could of Key West;
Soon we boarded a tender
Like potatoes in a blender
Arriving safely on shore—we were blest.

We sought out a trolley,
Everyone was quite jolly
In eager anticipation of the ride;
We passed Hemingway's house
And Hog's Breath Tavern where he
soused
Lush greenery grew on all sides.

Audubon's place loomed ahead,
Much about him was said
As our one hour tour sped on;
Truman's Little White House,
About the size of a mouse
Boasted of hardly any lawn.

An object shaped like a buoy
That resembled a toy
Was really an historical marker,
Citing the spot
As far as the USA got,
In the most seemly place they could park
her.

Touring Key West was brief

But caused us no grief
As we were driven along in grand style;
Here people of fame
Had embellished their names
While pursuing their dreams all the while.

Another tender ride
And we were inside
In a line at the welcoming Lido;
"My heavens, what a spread!"
These profound words were said
As the chefs endeavored to feed all.

After a little short rest
I began a quest
To learn about dinner utensils;
And found to my chagrin
I'd used the wrong spoon again—
Oh, where was my note pad and pencil?

The captain's reception,
Was a formal connection,
So we primped and patted with care;
Captain Dirk van den Berg
Was as good as his word,
He shook hands with everyone there.

I'd pictured him to be
A rugged man of the sea
With perhaps a beard and a pipe,
But this burly young fellow
Was clever and mellow,
My image of him was pure tripe.

Waiters moved to and fro
To keep champagne aflow,
Almost five hundred were there
Most had both style and class;
And and as they emptied their glass
They drank with abandon and flair.

The glamour and glitter
Had me all atwitter
Eyeing the grand gowns and suits;

I considered our past,
Felt we'd made it, at last.
This shebang was a rip-roarin' hoot.

We had just gotten seated
When we were greeted
With a cake meant especially for me!
Pete, in honor of my birth,
Sang for all he was worth,
For it was my birthday, you see.

Immediately thereafter
I burst into laughter,
When a bevy of waiters—there were four—
Sang *Happy Birthday* again;
Though their voices didn't blend
As they all hailed from foreign Singapore!

Entertainment that night
Was just exactly right,
A singer and a comedian supreme;
What a full day we'd had!
We were more than just glad
To sack out and hope for good dreams.

A new day arrived,
We were tired but alive,
We charted our day with delight;
I lost at Ring Toss,
Folded napkins like "the boss."
And Scrabble was way out of sight.

An early lunch was in store
Then we scooted out the door
For Cozumel, our p.m. destination;
The heat was intensive,
Most items were expensive,
So we guzzled a cola creation.

A colorful street
Lined with shops that looked neat
Belied the poverty that lay 'round the bend;

The windows were barred,
The restrooms all scarred,
To live here you'd be pressed to mend.

Nothing struck our fancy
Since values seemed chancy
And, besides, we had an urgent need,
I was seeking black coral
But felt I'd find it tomorrow,
So I failed to acknowledge their greed.

At dinner that night,
Tropical casual was right
Creating a relaxed atmosphere;
Later, by the pool
The night air was cool
As a funfest of games started there.

The seats were all taken
And our feet were achin'
As line dancers did *Alley Cat*;
Pete was feeling quite tough
And said he'd had enough
So we ended our day—that was that!

Tuesday at sea
Brought activities—
Port talks on Jamaica and Cayman;
Though Pete was quite dour,
He took a kitchen tour
And returned with stories aflamin'.

A contest was going
Where we would be showing
The number of miles we had gone?
I guessed two hundred seven,
And missed by more than eleven,
And that great big old ship traveled on.

I bought one card for Bingo
And enjoyed the quaint lingo
Of Gary who read off the dice;
His attempts to be funny,
At first did seem sunny,

But repetition landed him on thin ice.

Then we sat out on deck
So we could inspect
The ice-carving skills of the chefs;
With chisels and forks
Their skills were uncorked
Awesome! And our speech, it just left!

A dolphin! My word!
Then a rabbit and bird
Appeared before our very eyes;
They were quite clever
As they did endeavor
To create this chilling surprise.

The casino did beckon
And, as you might reckon,
I tried out my skill at the slots;
A few dings and clatters—
Something was the matter,
A mere pittance is all that I got!

That night after dinner
Again I was thinner—
The menu was worse every time;
Some thought it was great
And ate—my! They really ate!
While I just composed nasty rhymes.

The show that came later
Seemed even greater
Than the last one we'd seen in the hall;
Jamie Stewart sang
Till the entire room rang—
He provided great pleasure for all.

Comedian David Reid
Fulfilled our dire need
For relaxation and masterful wit;
This day in review--
Should have been two (days)—
We wouldn't have minded one bit.

Wednesday soon came
We abandoned all games,
Ocho Rios (in Jamaica) beckoned to us;
A tractor-drawn cart
That jerked from the start
Took us all around without fuss.

On the road to a farm
We met with no harm
But small, shabby homes and tin shacks
Made us wonder how they live
Close as holes in a sieve
With only ragged clothes on their backs.

Tropical flowers
Lined the roadways in bowers
In between patches of plants,
Anemic-looking fields
Offered up paltry yields
Returns on their crops are quite scant.

Cocoa, coffee, and cane,
Were viewed through the rain,
Bananas and orchids stood proud;
With offerings such as these
It was hard to believe
The poverty that does enshroud.

We saw a man
With his bare feet and hands
Climb straight up a thirty foot palm;
The feat was quite daring
But the man seemed uncaring,
Throughout, he was totally calm.

A coconut was broken
And, as a small token,
Small pieces were passed all around;
The white crunchy treat
Was tasty and sweet.
Munching was the prevailing sound.

Soon after, on a bus,
That would take all of us

To the famous Dunn's River Falls;
We caught glimpses along
Of an economy gone wrong
As our guide spoked of grand shopping
malls!

Dunn's River Flowed nefariously
As we perched precariously
On the walkway surrounding the edge;
It was both wet and cool
And we saw many fools
Climbing the rocks ledge by ledge.

The merchants around us
Brutally did hound us
Hawking their colorful wares;
We couldn't wait
To pass through the gate
To avoid their sad eyes and stares.

In the p.m.
We went out again
And crossed the long pier to the shore;
The Taj Mahal Mall
Seemed prosperous and all,
Barred windows told us even more.

Thirty per cent
Of all residents
Lack any means of survival,
Emotions are intensive,
Crimes are offensive—
Jamaica needs one grand revival.

We could hardly talk
As we continued our walk,
Accosted by cabbies galore;
Soni Mall came into view,
As we entered, we two,
Grateful for the safety of the stores.

Black coral was elusive
Though my search was profusive,
Methinks they don't have any here;

We turned our tired feet
Toward the heat of the street,
Our passage invoked many stares.

At dinner that night,
Clad elegantly right,
Dutch hats were found on our plates;
Richard placed mine just right
And, my! What a sight!
We balanced them carefully while we ate.

Immediately thereafter,
We followed the laughter
To the Crow's Nest in utter delight;
In a Sherlock Holmes game
One placed the blame
And ended the play for that night.

Show time was great
But we couldn't wait
To crawl into our little dinky bunks;
Pete left me quite early
But I felt that surely
My head would not nod or dunk.

There was a Filipino show,
The food workers, you know,
Who sang of their native land;
One dancer lost a 'breast'
From the area of his chest—
A balloon that was passed hand to hand.

Next day quite early,
We were both somewhat surly,
There never was enough time to sleep;
We arose and got dressed
Hoping for the best
Moving as fast as we could creep.

The Nieuw Amsterdam docked
But we were not shocked,
The Grand Caymans hove early into view;
We rode to George Town
Which we knew was renowned—

Five hundred banks! Give or take one or
two.
I carefully took aim,
As shopping was my game,
And studied the lay of the land;
We buzzed through the shops
As fast as we could hop
Comparing items, both cheap and quite
grand.

Fancy jewelry bewitched
On this island for the rich,
Prince Charles and Di had shopped there;
One store displayed
A black coral array
Of silver the couple purchased with care.

Only one shop
Made me seriously stop
And actually buy—not just look,
Earrings and a hat,
Some beads, that was that,
And, finally, a couple of books.

Then it was back to the ship
For a snack and a nip,
Soon we returned for a tour;
Our guide wasn't bright
We didn't see many sights
Our outlook remained somewhat dour.

With envelopes in hand
We went in a band
To a post office located...we-e-ll,
To our family and friends
We wanted to send
Greetings postmarked from HELL!

A turtle farm came next,
The odor somewhat vexed
As it pungently made itself known;
We saw turtles in stages
From young to old ages
At which time the stench was full-blown.

Georgetown was ranked
With all of its banks
As a crime-free island indeed;
No welfare was given
So citizens were driven
To work to satisfy their needs.

Jobs of any kind,
Were easy to find,
For all who wanted to work;
Drivers caught drinking
Had no time for blinking,
Their licenses were revoked if they
shirked.

The contrast between here
And Jamaica so near
Was infinitely hard to believe;
Cayman splendor was grand
Throughout the land,
While Jamaicans wore their hearts on
their sleeves.

That night we dressed formally,
Looked more elegant than normally,
Then I tried the casino again;
We had only a minute,
But I just had to spin it,
And hey, $95 I win!

As dinner progressed,
We could only guess
Why no dessert menus were shown;
Then, my! What a fright!
They extinguished the lights,
The reason totally unknown.

Chefs and waiters entered the room
From out of the gloom
In a glittering, sparkling parade;
One went to each table
As quickly as able

And served Baked Alaskas they'd made.

At show time that night,
The mood was just right
For a breathtaking, fast-moving show,
Double Trouble was their name
And juggling was their game,
Twins who threw pins! What a show!

Friday at sea,
Between you and me,
Seemed to have a leisurely pace;
Boy, was I wrong,
Time marched right along
As we ended our trip like a race.

I was so hungry that day
That I didn't delay
But ate breakfast alone by myself;
A lady who bumped me
Spilled coffee, you see,
Like a visit from a very bad elf.

As nine-o-clock came
I picked up a game
Which was called a Picture Puzzle Quiz;
I worked for a bit
Then gave up on it
As time moved on like a whiz.

Morning Madness came next,
This treasure hunt perplexed
As teams raced to find certain objects;
It was approached seriously
And pursued quite deliriously,
Contestants were excited, I expect.

Then the time came
For a change of pace frame--
Information on disembarkation;
The procedure seemed clear
But brought me no cheer,
The trip seemed of quite short duration.

Bingo grimly ensued,
The crowd was subdued,
Pursuing a prize of one grand;
No one was lucky
But that was just ducky,
At least it hadn't gotten out of hand.

We ate and then packed—
Many items were stacked
As we filled our cases to the brim;
Then at one forty-five
I said, "Man alive!"
The Electric Slide was performed once
again.

Two-thirty arrived
Hordes thronged to the hive,
Horse racing fun soon began;
The jockeys and nags
Wore similar rags
Some had collected their fans.

Bets were soon placed
For each race that was raced,
Bedlam ensued—what a roar!
Cheer leaders yelled
At each sound of the bell,
With a different horse at the fore.

Number six raced ahead
Past the others he sped
Causing a rip–roaring conclusion;
We were glad we'd escaped
With nary a rape—
Not even a bloody contusion.

Jackpot Bingo came then,
Someone would win
Even if 'twas played through the night;
Twenty-four hundred dollars
Was pursued by us "scholars"
Each claiming to win was his right.

I had three squares to go

When two loud "B-I-N-G-O-S"
Rang out as clear as a bell;
Some of us groaned
While others just moaned--
Disgruntled, we muttered, "Oh, well."

A talent show followed
That should have stayed bottled—
Two men cracked timeworn show
stoppers;
But another made claim
To be his own grandpa of fame
But the egg that he laid was a whopper.

One lady, alone,
Ascended the throne
With a vocal rendition of fame;
Her *Indian Love Call*
Did crack and then fall,
Some said they were sorry she came.

We hurried to our room
Like a race in full bloom
And finished the rest of our packing;
We shoved our bags in the hall
Then stood proud and tall
As many places with luggage were
lacking.

We showered and dressed
And went out in quest
Of gifts on sale in the shops;
The gifts that I found
Had the best prices around
On this night they'd pulled out the stops.

We needed some food—
Didn't want to be rude
So we went to the high–up Crow's Nest;
We hoped for hors d'oeuvres
Not many were served
But the sunset we saw was the best.

Our last dinner on board
Evened the score,
Finally, a *decent* prime rib!
Our waiter even smiled,
Seemed almost beguiled
That, at last, I'd staked out my dibs.

All during the week
I'd turned the other cheek
While some had escargot and caviar;
But American red meat
Was a far better treat
It outdid those delicacies by far.

Our whole dining group
Left in a troop
For the Newlywed Game in the hall;
Though remarks were kept clean
Innuendos were gleaned
We laughed till we cried one and all.

The last show we saw
Was the best one of all,
Jamie Stewart sang out his heart;
David Reid came,
Gave us more of the same,
We guffawed at him from the start.

We fell into bed
Barely touching our heads
When our alarm sounded the start
Of our last groans and sighs
As we said our goodbyes
To this cruise of which we were a part.

Every short minute
Had much pleasure in it,
It was truly a real life adventure;
The whole trip had seemed
Like a really real dream.
Would I hear someone say,
"GO AHEAD! PINCH HER?!!!"

This was the poem we sent to our friends and family from Hell in the Cayman Islands.

THE SMITHS SAY HELL-O
1994

Exemplary lives we thought we had led,
But here we are, and we're not even dead!
All we can say is, "Well, do tell!
It seems we've landed here in HELL!"
If you should sail the Holland Line,
You'd see that HELL can be quite fine.

****

OUR CHRISTMAS LETTER FOR 1994

What a year '94 has been!
Glad we won't ever live it again.
Pete's puny heart and the bypass
correction
Made for tense moments—an iffy
connection.

However, it seems he weathered it well
And, in the fall, we cruised down to Hell;
Please do take note, 'twas the Hell on
Grand Cayman,
NOT the one in the Bible—no NOT the
SAME one.

We also added a third generation
On March 31st—Tim and Lisa's creation—
A new baby boy has graced our small
group
And we now comprise a quite hefty
troupe.

This pregnancy was dubious even from
the first
All the way through it, we expected the
worst;
Though Lisa and the baby had a difficult
time,

Both emerged in good health spawning
this happy rhyme.

Our group totals six, but Lori swears there
are seven;
She says she believes two babies came
from Heaven.
Wayne is the one who giggles and coos—
Evil twin Whine, WHINES, and gives us
the blues.

This year we have reached the very tip-
top,
Good fortune has smiled and pulled out
the stops.
Our group is intact even though we
scraped bottom,
We thank the one above, because we've
still got 'em.

Tim has become a conglomerate
corporation
For he's doing just about every job in the
nation;
He's a husband, a father, a housekeeper,
and a nanny
Writing his dissertation and working off
his fanny.

We wish you and yours nothing but the BEST,
A VERY MERRY CHRISTMAS and all of the rest

A very happy new year, A VERY JOYOUS TIME,
And this is the end of this pitiful rhyme.

****

HAPPY BIRTHDAY, NATALIE
March 1995

No need to worry,
No need to fret,
With each passing day
'Tis older we get;

Enjoy with great gladness
Each sunrise anew
And remember—
      GOD made it—
Especially for YOU.

HAPPY BIRTHDAY, NATALIE #2
March 1995

So limber are your fingers,
So nimble are your toes,
That you can make sweet music
Where e'r you choose to go.

With fingers always ready
To tap a tune or two
And toes abouncin' almost off
You take your washboard cue.

The rapid rhythms beat wildly beat,
Crescendos rise, then fall,
Pianissimos and fortissimos?
You can play them all.

It's hard to really reckon
The accolades to your great name
For you are ONLY SEVENTY
Just starting your walk to fame.

So happy birthday, to you Nat,
We hope you'll have a ball
As you embark upon your trip
To play at CARNEGIE HALL!

Here's a ruffle for your collar,
A buckle for your shoe,
A thimble for you finger,
But the rest is up to you.

KATHY OBIE TURNS 50
March 25, 1995

Thank you for the party,
The dancing and the fun,
'Twas quite a lively evening
Even strenuous for some.

The ladies looked so lovely
In their cowboy hats with bows
Their fancy fringe and laces
And their booted scootin' toes.

117

Even old St. Paddy
Would doff his hat and grin,

"For-r-r a lass who's just turned 50,
'Tis pr-r-retty good shape ye'r-r-r in!"

HAPPY BIRTHDAY, TIM
9-2-95

Even though these words come late,
The message is still timely,
We hope year 36 is great
And things proceed sublimely.

It takes a special kind of man
To be a Mr. Mom,
To change the diapers 'n' all that stuff
And wipe up the goop and gom.

All your efforts, dear son-in-law,
From one end to the other,
Are appreciated the very most
By both Lisa and her mother.

Grandpa Wayne is quite content
And applauds the work you do;
He just sits back in his rocking chair
Thankful it's NOT HIM—BUT YOU!

HAPPY BIRTHDAY, LISA
1-16-96

Once again the time is here
To wish you happy birthday, dear,

Time to think of the year just passed
That has made you a mother, at last...
          AT LAST!

Time to rejoice, to celebrate anew,
What a wonderful treasure we have in
you.

*See below—optional insert

May all the birthdays that come your way
Be as richly blessed as this one today.

*Time for me to remember *your* dirty
diapers
And smugly observe who now pays the
piper!

HAPPY BIRTHDAY, WAYNE
1996

Blessings on thee, child of two,
Here's Grandma and Grandpa talking to
you.
To both of us you've brought much joy,
But, then, you're just a very young boy.

As you grow older we're keeping score
And hoping to add on many, many, many
more
HAPPY, HAPPY BIRTHDAYS!

THE SWEET SONG OF THE FROG
1996
(For Wayne P. Brakel for Easter)

Two Easter bunnies
Came hopping this way
One said, "Let's leave Wayne
Some pretty eggs today."

They sat for a while
On the top of a log
When what should appear
But a very big frog!

He saw them and croaked
In his very BIG voice,
"R-r-r-rib-bit   r-r-r-ribit,"
Were the words of his choice.

Then right at the end,
This very big bloke
Sang one final "R-r-r-ribit"
And a great big loud CR-O-O-O-A-A-AK!"

And the wee little bunnies
Thought they would just die
As they laughed and they laughed
Till tears came to their eyes.

"Please come with us
Sing your song to young Wayne,
He lives over there
Down a very long lane."

Wayne looked out of the window
And saw quite a sight—
Two Easter bunnies
In early morn's light.

The frog was a big one
And he sat by a tree

But the grass was quite tall
So Wayne could not see.

The bunnies dropped eggs
As they hopped over the grass
While Wayne pressed his nose
On the clear window glass.

He watched and he listened;
This is what he heard
Even at age two
He thought it absurd.

Hop, hop, "Rr-r-ribit"
Drop, drop, "CR-0-0-0AK"
Wayne laughed and he giggled
Till his parents awoke.

Over and over
The frog sang his song—
Wayne really liked it
And sang right along.

"Hop. hop. "r-r-rr-bit
Drop, drop, CR- O–A-K!"
What a strange Easter song
He sang to his folks!

Mom and Dad had to tell him
The truth of the thing,
A frog makes those sounds
And bunnies don't sing.

Nevertheless,
Each Easter thereafter,
Wayne remembered that song
And giggled with laughter.

Carolyn Krebs was my husband's secretary for many years at Oxford School in Oxford, Indiana. This was written for her retirement.

CONGRATULATIONS CAROLYN KREBS
1996

For all of these years
You've kept things straight—
Principal and teachers
And parents irate.

Students, loud and noisy,
Racing through the hall,
Your records have been perfect
And you've answered every call.

You've duly done your duty
And in the years to come
You need a brand new interest

So life won't be humdrum.

Here's a bit of worthy advice
So life will smoothly flow,
ALWAYS STRIVE TO KEEP YOUR DUCKS
IN A COMPLETELY PERFECT ROW.

Ducks, like kids, do wander
As they waddle to and fro,
But we have learned the secret,
And we want you to know.
        HAVE ONLY ONE DUCK!
(Clarence. Her husband.)

****

In 1996 I was asked to write an introduction for a play entitled, *Charge It, Please*. It was performed by the drama group at Scottish Highlands in Leesburg, Florida. Pete (Wayne) and I lived in that retirement community from 1990 to 2007.

THE WORD CHARGE

I was asked to introduce to you
The play you came to see,
But I was told I must not say
Just what the play would be.

Therefore, I'll just present to you
Loose thoughts about this word;
You'll hear it in the play tonight
It's one you've no doubt heard.

You read it in a poem
Called *The CHARGE of the Light Brigade*;
You also learned in history
That armies CHARGED when they were
bade.

You saw it every day at school
When teachers were in CHARGE,
And felt it when the wink of an eye
Produced a CHARGE quite large,

You experienced it when you grew up
And suddenly—you were the one!
Now in CHARGE of YOUR OWN LIFE,
What happened to all the fun?

The cast tonight is all CHARGED up
With energy and emotion;
I wonder what CHARGE will mean to
them,
Have you really any notion?

I think that we are ready now
So without any further ado,

We proudly present, *CHARGE It, Please*,
We've prepared it just for you.

****

The following poems were written for our neighbors' (Frank and Natalie Biesinger) 50th Wedding anniversary. I served as master of ceremonies and read them aloud.

THE PROPOSAL
1996

He gazed into her deep blue eyes
Begging, "Will you please marry me?"
She said, "I might if you could learn
To do it properly."

He was alarmed and so aghast
He stuttered shamelessly,
"B-B-But, love I did! I DID say please
As has been taught to me."

Demurely, she looked up at him,
Her lashes swept her cheek,
She studied him disdainfully.
Then slowly did she speak.

"I know, my love, you did say please.
Quite nicely was your question put,
What I don't see is bended knee!
You are standing on my foot!!!"

WEDDING PRAYERS
1996

They stood there at the altar,
The preacher said, "Let's pray."
So each one did as had been asked
But each in his own way.

Nat thought ahead of her future with Frank
Then prayed fervently with care,

"I know Frank's hair is not the best
But, please Lord, leave it all there."

Frank prayed, "Lord, I'm just a man,
I know I'm not worthy of Nat,
Please give her all the help you can
Don't turn her ugly and fat."

THAT MOMENT OF TRUTH
1996

The wedding now was over
The guests had gone away,
All that was left were the gifts and the mess
And the memories of that day.

Nat looked at Frank, and he at her.
They were just too tired to speak
They sat a while in silence
Embracing cheek to cheek.

Then, after a while, the truth sank in,
THEY WERE NOW HUSBAND AND WIFE!

And...I don't know why it happened that way,
But they SUDDENLY....CAME TO LIFE!!!!!

ON KEEPING YOUR DUCKS IN A ROW*
1996

Fifty years of marriage
With fifty more to come,
You need a brand new interest
So life won't be humdrum.

Here's a bit of worthy advice
So life will smoothly flow
Always strive to keep your ducks
In a completely perfect row.

Ducks, you know, do wander
As they waddle to and fro,
But we have learned the secret
And we want you to know.

HAVE ONLY ONE DUCK! (Frank)

(*I also used his same poem when Pete's secretary retired from Oxford School.)

For Cathy Obie and her two friends, who I had hired to line dance at the Biesinger's 50th Wedding Anniversary dinner. February 1996 at Vic's Embers in Leesburg, Florida.

YOU'RE THE CAT'S MEOW
1996

Thank you for your kindness;
You've helped in your own way
To make this golden wedding date
A very special day.

Your dances were truly terrific;
The tunes were toe-tapping stuff;
Now, is it any wonder
That even WE have lost our puff?

For Joe Perkovic and wife, whom I had hired to be strolling violinists at the Biesinger 50th Wedding Anniversary dinner. February 1996 at Vic's Embers.

THANKS FOR TUNING A MEMORABLE EVENT
1996

Thank you for your kindness;
You've helped in your own way
To make his golden wedding date
A very special day.

Tonight we Love was beautiful;
For Nat and Frank it was a treat;
It added one more memory
To make their "golden day" complete.

While my husband and I were living in Oxford, we were asked one year to chaperone the high school prom. That experience was the basis for this poem.

MY HIGH SCHOOL PROM
July 13, 1997

High school graduation came,
The prom was yet to be.
Most other girls had snagged a beau.
I too was asked, you see.

I dressed so very carefully
In a flowing dancing gown.
My hair was clean and shining
With tresses tumbling down.

A ruffly, frilly cape enclosed
My shoulders lean and bare.
I knew I looked my grandest.

I'd dressed with utmost care.

In great anticipation,
I heard the doorbell ring.
And, lo, he'd sent me flowers
With pretty bows 'n' things.

My date was spiffed up nicely
When he appeared upon the scene.
'Twas then a small voice said brightly,
"Mom, you forgot your wedding ring!"

*****

I sent this to all of The Loch Ness Monsters when we moved from Scottish Highlands to the Royal Oak Estates while our house was being built in The Villages.

123

WHEN ALL OF THE JOKING IS OVER
November 12, 1997

When all of the joking is over,
When all of the pranks have been played,
Consider it our way of saying
Thank you, we're glad that you've stayed.

Now, before we get all maudlin

With eyes puddling up, lookin' sad,
Remember the gist of this poem...
Is, Hey! You guys ain't doin' too bad.

Stay healthy and keep on truckin'!

Top row: Leona Smith, Toni Kartye, Natalie Biesinger. Bottom row: Barb Jones, Betty Pfau.

CHAPTER 3
ROYAL OAK ESTATES
Leesburg, Florida

Since we planned to return to Indiana,
We holed up in a town house to wait
For an apartment in Indianapolis
At a retirement home that we knew was great.

I filled my days with music,
Organ classes at Fletcher's [a music store at Lake Square Mall] were a dream,
I wrote many musical pieces—
Composing is tougher than it seems.

The music that I wrote inspired me
To write a musical play,
Jamie's Roses was born to fight boredom
And I did it all my own way.

In February of 1997 we sold our home at Scottish Highlands in Leesburg, Florida. Because of Wayne's five heart bypasses surgery in 1994 and the installment of his pacemaker in 1996, we decided it would be best for us to go into a retirement home in Indianapolis, Indiana. While we were on the waiting list for Marquette Manor, we moved into a town house at Royal Oak Estates in Leesburg. After several months of waiting, we decided to take one last look at similar retirement facilities in the central Florida area. We were on our way to Ocala when we drove past The Villages. Wayne suggested we stop and have a look at the new additions there. We did more than just look. We bought a lot and signed a contract to have another home built. We moved into that home on November 12, 1997. While we were at Royal Oak Estates I wrote the play mentioned above, which isn't included here, and the poems below.

A friend of mine gave me a list of old adages. I thought it would be fun to interpret them in a different in a way that I knew was not meant to be. Several of these were published in 1997 in the nearby Villages newspaper, *The Daily Sun*. I usually submitted them to the newspaper in groups of three or four. When one group was submitted, the editor at that time listed then as "Addled Adages." I thought it was a good name, so here they are, my version of "Addled Adages."

WORDS OF WISDOM

Words of wisdom
Should be remembered and used
To make life's journey finer.

Too often they're tucked away inside a book
With beautiful pages and binder.

IN DUE TIME

"In due time" is a phrase
That often is used
Whenever specifics are lacked.
"In due time" time
Stre-e-e-tches further ahead
And ne-e-ever seems to come back.
Whatever was promised "in due time,"
alas, is forgot!
And never thereafter is mentioned.

THE TIME OF DAY

"I wouldn't give him the time of day!"
Are words spat out as a threat.
Not to worry if he has the same thought
of you
And coins YOUR OWN EPITHET.

THE EARLY BIRD GETS THE WORM

The early bird gets the worm?
It sounds all well and good,
But, what if I'm an ole woodpecker
'N' I'd rather peck on wood?

PATIENCE IS A VIRTUE

Patience is a virtue
A belief that is surely sublime
Unless you are waiting
At the end of the line.

A PENNY FOR YOUR THOUGHTS

When I am deep in contemplation
And someone says this phrase to me,
"A penny for your thoughts?"
I gaze on him disparagingly.

"A penny? My good man!
What a paltry fee!
If that's all you can pay,

I'll keep my thoughts to me!"

A STITCH IN TIME SAVES NINE

"A stitch in time saves nine," we've heard
But how can anyone know?
If one stitch is taken,
Then some may be saved,
But will the number of those lost ever
show?

A PENNY SAVED IS A PENNY EARNED

Another wise saying
Was coined long ago,
I'll tell you quite simply
It doesn't seem so.

If I find a coin lying lost in the street—
The owner makes no claim,
We never meet—
Can't I save that penny
Without having earned it?
There's a deep lesson here
But I've never learned it.

BIRDS OF A FEATHER FLOCK TOGETHER

Birds of a feather flock together.
What astounding insight I see!
Of course those bare birds will flock
together
How else to keep warm with *only* one
feather?

DON'T BURN YOUR BRIDGES BEHIND YOU

"Don't burn your bridges behind you."
You've heard this a thousand times,
But the only bridges that I own
I'll tell you about in a rhyme—
        No preamble
        Non-flammable!

A BIRD IN THE HAND IS WORTH TWO IN
THE BUSH

With a bird in my hand
It would be my wish
To send that bird sailing
Away on his tush.

With an attitude like that,
I'll never discover
The value of those two
Who have taken cover.

SEE A PIN PICK IT UP, ALL THAT DAY
YOU'LL HAVE GOOD LUCK

I saw a pin upon the floor
As I was flying through the door.
But, lo, I stopped and I did duck
To claim my token of good luck.
Then I questioned why I'd lingered
Since all I got was one pricked finger.

SEEING IS BELIEVING

If seeing is believing
Then I must need new eyes,
For it's still UNbelivable to me
That tiny little birds can fly.

FOOLS RUSH IN WHERE ANGELS FEAR TO
TREAD
Fools rush in
Where angels fear to tread—
If this is true,
The thing I dread.

Is that someday
When I've fallen low
No angels will appear
They'll be too scared to go!

Will some fool rush in?
Mother, have mercy!

If he truly is a fool
He'll probably only curse me.

A WATCHED POT NEVER BOILS

"A watched pot never boils"
Has been repeated forever,
But was he who coined it
Really so clever?

My family would suffer,
Perhaps grow quite thin,
If the pots that I've watched
Couldn't even begin.

IF WISHES WERE FISHES,
WE'D DINE EVERY DAY

"If wishes were fishes,
We'd dine every day."
But where would we sit?
Where would we play?

The world would be filled
With catfish and herring
And swordfish and sharks,
Both vicious and daring.

And, after a while,
We'd be buried alive
With those stinky old fishes
Our minds had contrived.

Then eat them each day?
Not in my book!
I'd be off and away
Seeking veggies to cook.

EARLY TO BED, EARLY TO RISE,
MAKES A MAN HEALTHY,
WEALTHY AND WISE

What if one night
I bed down at seven,

Should I arise when I wake
At half past eleven?

Will I then be more healthy,
More wealthy and wise?
No! I'll just need the bathroom,
As you may surmise.

WHAT GOES ROUND COMES ROUND

If a rocket revolves
Several times round the earth,
Then crashes in ashes
In a fiery mountain berth,

Will it again come around
To the point where it started
When its innards and workings
Have all now departed?

I think, not my dear,
It won't come round again,
For it's now all in pieces
In the place that it's in.

RED SKY AT NIGHT, SAILOR'S DELIGHT, RED SKY AT MORNING, SAILORS TAKE WARNING.

"Red sky at night, sailor's delight,"
Of course that old salt's in a tizzy!
The poor guy worked hard the livelong
day
Until he is giddy, quite dizzy.

"Red sky at morning, sailors take
warning."
Each day's a nefarious gamble
Will Neptune be waiting to swallow him
up?
Will wild winds leave his ship in a
shambles?

WE'LL CROSS THAT BRIDGE WHEN WE COME TO IT

"We'll cross that bridge."
When? One might ask,
Even though it seems
A very small task.

The answer we're told
Is,"When we come to it."
Now, I kindly ask
As a mostly sane friend,

"Did you think we might cross it
Before it begins?"

YOU CAN'T HAVE YOUR CAKE AND EAT IT TOO

"You can't have your cake
And eat it too."
Is one old saying
That's surely not true.

I MUST have cake
If I am to eat it;
This logic's so bad
I wouldn't repeat it!

THERE'S MORE THAN ONE WAY TO SKIN A CAT

"There's more than one way to skin a
cat."
You've heard it said before
But when I think of that cat's fur
I shudder more and more.

I'm just a softie
Who has never recovered
From the three little kittens
Who one day discovered
That their mittens were lost
And went crying to their mother.

A JOURNEY OF A THOUSAND MILES
STARTS WITH THE FIRST STEP

If you were leaving on a journey,
Would it really seem quite clever
To start with, maybe...step twenty-two?
 Well, I never ever!

LET SLEEPING DOGS LIE

"Let sleeping dogs lie"
Is rather strange advice
Since everyone knows
That lying isn't nice.

But, what if a dog
Told lies galore?
If he wagged his cute tail,
I'd want to hear more.

LET SLEEPING DOGS LIE

"Let sleeping dogs lie?"
But, of course, we will.
Did you think they might sleep
While running uphill?

HASTE MAKES WASTE

First I was a teacher,
Then I was a wife.
Then I was a mother;
All had stress and strife.

"Haste makes waste"

Simply doesn't fit,
If I hadn't worked in haste
I'll still be doing it!

If my speed made waste,
I learned to use it, too,
So don't admonish me
Or I'll do the same to you.

****

HALLOWEEN MANIA
1997

Halloween witches flying on brooms,
Jack-o-lanterns grinning big—
Even grown-ups prancing about
In the most unseemly rigs.

Apples and cider and donuts and stuff,
Parades and costumes galore,
All I can say is I l-o-o-v-e- it.
Give me more, give me more, GIVE ME
MORE!

129

CHAPTER 4
THE VILLAGES
Lady Lake, Florida

The Villages was our third location,
Since leaving the state of our roots,
The good times in Florida continued
With the worst of times thrown in to boot

Wayne survived leukemia and diabetes,
Our lives became more sedate;
The good times were ours for the taking—
The Villages earned our best rate.

Now we met people from abroad,
From Ireland, Great Britain and such,
Many envied us for our homeland
Because it offered so much.

We had moved two times in one year and to top off that record, I fell and broke my left arm just three weeks before the second move. Somehow we made it without any outside help other than the moving company. Thus began another brand new life with a whole new set of people to know and write about.

I continued writing poems while Pete's activities had considerably shrunk. I spent my time going to movies and eating out (when Pete felt up to it). I line danced, played Bingo, Bunco, and Pokeno. Life was still pretty good because we could see NASA shuttles being thrust into space from our own lanai!

I wrote the following poem for Norman and Sallie Pokinghorn, the neighbors who kept our house key while we were away in the summer of 1998.

THE KEEPER OF THE KEY
1998

We thank you neighbors for the feat,
The keeping of the key,
Please know that we're appreciative
And thank you heartily.

Our new neighbors, Mike and Malcine Maher, from Ireland, hosted a Halloween party.

HALLOWEEN THANKS
1998

We thank you kindly neighbors
For inviting us to share
This time of pure tom-foolery
Being as silly as we dare.

Of all the people we have known
You rank among the best
In playing your roles superbly
As perfect host and hostess.

****

THANKSGIVING
(Appeared in The Villages *Daily Sun* 1999)

Thanksgiving is a time of thanks
For blessings we've received
But, what if there was a payback?
Could our debts ever be relieved?

THANKSGIVING #2
(Appeared in The Villages *Daily Sun* 1999)

Thanksgiving comes but once each year
But, perhaps that shouldn't be.
Each day brings to the fore,
Much, much more
To be appreciated thankfully.

****

THANK YOU, ROSE
1999

I thank you kindly, Rose
For your efforts on our behalf,
For all of the dances taught patiently,
And for sometimes making us laugh.

So rhythmic are your cha-cha-chas.
So graceful are your vines,

So dainty are your shuffles
When viewed from the behind.

We can only try to imitate
Your snip-snap-snappy routines,
Perhaps we'll polka right out of here
And become real live dancing machines.

I took a plate of coconut balls and mint cookies to a line dancing Christmas party. I wrote this poem to go with them but the table was so crowded that I couldn't place it beside the goodies as I had planned. This appeared in The Villages *Daily Sun* 5-19-02. I had submitted it to the *Daily Sun* just before Christmas of 2001—A Christmas poem in May?!!!

COCONUT BALLS AND MINT COOKIES
1999

Coconut balls and mint cookies
Seem quite appropriate to me
How many times have you dieted
To become the best you could be?

We're nearing the end of the century!
You owe it to yourself!
Please indulge in some chocolate,
I don't want it left on MY shelf!

****

When I joined The Villages Computer Club, one of the members who helped me the most was Maxine Miller from Atlanta, Georgia. She was club president. She often sent out tips to anyone who signed up for them, which I did. The tips were invaluable.

MAX THANKS
2000

I thank you kindly Max
For all your timely tips,
And for the spiritual enlightenment
That kept us really hip.

I know that my computer
Would dearly love to say,
"Y'all helped me to keep healthy,
Now, don't y'all go away."

I'M JUST A COMPUTER
(Appeared in *The Daily Sun* 1-23-2000)

Although I'm just a computer,
One little old machine,
I know that I am a giant
That can make y'all turn green.

I can create a beautiful greeting,
Find facts for you until dawn,
In fact, my list of abilities
Runs on and on and on.

My powers are so awesome,
I can travel the world in a flash,
I can send for you a letter
Or withdraw some personal cash.

My prowess is unlimited!
I can do everything I said,
And if you don't push the right buttons,
I can even make you turn red.

TOCHENY PARTY THANKS (Christmas Party 1999)
1999

Thank you kindly neighbors
For inviting us to share
Your holiday festivities
Prepared with such great care.

It's fun to be with people
Who know how to laugh and play,
Your party was the "topper"
Of another grand Florida day.

MEGYESI PARTY THANKS (New Year's Eve 1999)
1999

We thank you kindly Dot and Gene
For inviting us to share
In greeting the new millennium
With everybody there.

We'll store this night in memory
Of many best wishes and hugs
As we toasted the end of the century,
And END of that Y2K Bug!

THE FAN DANCER
(Appeared in *The Daily Sun* 9-10-2000)
2000

Sensuously she glides to the center,
Slowly stretches one arm in the air,
Her hand slides over a bauble
Which she gracefully handles with care.

Pleasure untold overtakes her
Filling her being with élan,
Perspiration rolls slowly, then falters,
As the dance continues on.

Reveling in rapturous enjoyment,
She glides to the center again.
Slowly stretches an arm toward the bauble,

Then she notices the place that she's in.

Mushrooms? *A can of mushrooms?*
She had really gotten carried away.
It seems she'd wound up in a pantry
On a hot, steamy, Florida day!!

No fans did she find in that closet,
No relief in there from the heat,
But the fan she'd turned on was a blessing!
In fact, Florida fans can't be beat.

A TRUE FLORIDA CRACKER
(Appeared in *The Villages Daily Sun* 10-22-2000)
2000

What is a true Florida Cracker?
Who coined this term long ago?

Some say Crackers were cowboys
Who cracked whips to make cattle go.

133

Others say Crackers were settlers
Who cracked corn to make grits and flour,
But anyone who is savvy knows the truth,
'Twas *Jimmy* who cracked corn by the
hour.

A true Florida Cracker is a lady
Who has basked and browned in the sun.

Her skin has darkened, changed colors,
Like toast she appears overdone.

Hubby knows not to hug his charred lady,
Like a cracker she may crumble and
break.
He'll bow his head fervently praying
That she won't do the same to his steak.

****

NEW YEAR'S RESOLUTIONS
(Appeared in *The Villages Daily* Sun 2-6-2000)
2000

New Year's resolutions are one thing
When your concerns are all about you,
But they are only a drop in the bucket
When compared with all that you view.

What would you resolve for your family?
Your community? Your city? Your state?
Your country? The world? The Universe?
Such resolutions would have to be great.

Could one mind even imagine
Resolutions to encompass all?
When considering the totality, the
masses,
Guess my personal resolutions are small,
    So...I'd really like...
            Just one more...
            Piece of cake,
And that's all.

HAPPY BIRTHDAY, LORI
August 18, 2000

May the road continue forward,
May the weight drop off in tons,
May fortune smile upon you
As you tighten up those buns.

May you always be a person
Who improves along the way
And may you have a perfectly perfect
Big red letter day!

****

The Villages Daily Sun asked subscribers to send birthday cards to honor Harold Schwartz, the founder of The Villages, on the occasion of his 90th birthday.

ODE IN AWE OF HAROLD SCHWARTZ
2000

Harold Schwartz is a dreamin' man;
He has dreamed more dreams

Than most any man can.

134

He has dreamed huge dreams
Then bigger dreams galore,
With each being greater
Than the one that came before.

We each stand in awe
Of this gracious man

Who included all of us
In his master plan.

May this year's celebration
Be the best you've ever got
'Cause 90 years of birthdays
Is a God-awful lot!

****

In August of 2000, Tim and Lisa moved from Ogden, Utah to Temperance, Michigan.

WELCOME TO YOUR NEW HOME
2000

Driving across country
With two lively boys in tow
Makes your arrival seem much sweeter
Though like houses stand all in a row.
Yours will become what you make it,
So go, kids, go!

****

THE LANGUAGES OF THE VILLAGES
2000

Words can befuddle and muddle
When isolated orations occur,
Few areas are as difficult to master
As the language of the English spoken
word.

Consider a line dancing lady
Being told to meringue and switch.
Vine right, vine left, but don't falter,
Do a Monterey spin and a hitch.

A new golfer claims rather loudly,
I birdied, and eagled, and scored,
I did it all with a fine iron!
At golfing, I never am bored!

Think of a line dancing lady

And this golfer who claims he had scored,
Each activity has its own language
Which participants cannot ignore.

Now, what I yearn to discover
Is a language of which I've heard tell,
That embodies quite strange innuendoes
And nothing's as clear as a bell.

With computers, it's defrag and scanner,
Modem, hard drive, and hack,
A mouse that I assume will counter
When a virus is about to attack.

I know the lingo of Bingo,
I know some of that line dancing stuff,
I have enough fragmented knowledge

135

To know that I don't have enough.

I can't help but sit here and wonder

How so many deviations could befall
Our perfectly good English language
That was once comprehended by all!

CHRISTMAS CARD FOR 2000
2000

Never, never, never
Have we ever, ever, ever,
Wished for you better Christmas than this.

Nor have we ever,
Never, never, never,
Sent to you A Happy New Year kiss!
So-o-o, here it iss!

****

Maxine Miller, president of The Villages Computer Club told us one day that she had seen a fox on the green while she and some friends were out golfing. I added some unseemly events to spice up the tale a bit and here it is!

A FOXY TALE (A 76% True Villages Tale)
2000

It seems that a lady
Of whom I've heard tell
One day played a golf game
And was doing quite well.

It is said that her ball
Landed thi-i-is close to the hole,
She would have birdied,
But, then, dontcha know?

One sly old fox
Was awaitin' from afar
And decided then and there
That HE'D be the star.

Like a flash from the heavens
He streaked by so fast

And he snatched up that ball
While the golfers all gasped.

Guess his ole worn out teeth
Weren't too strong,
Or, maybe he didn't like the taste
'Cause he dropped it before long

The lady lost the game
But so did the fox,
He wound up that day
In a little brown box.

And filchin' ole fox--
He just changed his role,
He still strolls the grounds—
In the shape of a stole!!

WHEN SPRING HAS SPRUNG
2000

When spring has sprung
And songs have been sung,
And blossoms hang heavy with dew;

When green grass appears
And everyone cheers,
My thoughts will all be of you.

For when the lawn dries
Under radiant skies
It needs your undivided attention.

The times will be few
To converse with you
There'll be more work than I can but mention.

A WALK ON THE FARM IN THE SPRINGTIME
2000

Spring, sprang, sprung,
Ding, dang, dung!

****

OH, VALENTINE, MY VALENTINE
A Valentine Vignette
1999

He: Oh, valentine, my valentine.
Won't you be my valentine?

She: Oh, yes, dear one,
I might be thine
I'd like to be your valentine.

He: And would you love and honor me
If I should beg on bended knee?

She: Perhaps if you would loyal be
And always love me just for me?

He: And would you keep my house, dear one
And cook for me when that is done?
And would you kindly tend my needs
And mow the yard and pull the weeds?

She: Oh, yes, I'll do those things for you
If you would kindly kiss my shoe.

MARCH
2000

March is a time of great wonder
As nature prepares for a change.

The weather can be wild and windy,
With so much new growth to arrange.

New buds, then blossoms and foliage,
New fruit, to grow heavy on limbs,
What raptures await the beholder
As the sun turns to twilight and dims.

The moon seems to shine even brighter
Dark images appear crystal clear,
Can life ever be any finer?
It's time to stand up and cheer!

YOUR JACK BENNY YEAR (For Lori Smith)
2001

This year, dear Lori Lynn,
Your perennial age has arrived,
Forever hereafter you can claim "39"--
Never must you be 45.

So try 39 for a year,
If it fits, use it forever,
Emulate Jack Benny who lied about his age
And was lauded for being quite clever.

HAPPY BIRTHDAY, TIM
2001

As sure as a vine winds around a tree,
'Tis one year older you must be.
One year older and, sad but true,
You have now reached 42.

Forty-two and still going strong,
Let's celebrate and sing this song:

Happy birthday to you,
Happy birthday to you,
Happy birthday dear Timothy,
You're now 42.

(And be very happy that I wasn't singing it, too!)

SPRING
2001

When flowers bloom
And robins sing
And kites fly high,
You'll know it's spring.

For a poetry contest for seniors in Wood County, Ohio, contestants were asked to write about "Life's Moments" to express the uniqueness of our journey in life. My entry was titled *An Unusual Surprise*. It is a true story that took place at Royal Oaks in Leesburg, Florida where I lived at the time.

AN UNUSUAL SURPRISE
2001

A bright orange sun painted the sky
Lifting my spirits way up high.
I walked my usual morning route
While a rooster cock-a-doodled his wake
up shout.

The mournful lowing of a needful cow
Lent its cadence to a hungry cat's meow.
When all of a sudden, I heard a "cat call"
whistle.
My head spun around with the speed of a
missile.

To hear that whistle at age sixty-seven?
I felt I had died and gone to heaven.

So-o-o I just *had* to know what man had
done this deed
At my advanced age, it was a powerful
need.

Quite soon I spied him, the culprit in
person,
'Twas then that my mood began to
worsen,
On a screened-in porch inside a cage he
sat
Bobbing his head to and fro like a sly old
cat!

I didn't care at all that my 'he' was a
parrot!!!
I had had my thrill—I would just grin and
bear it.

****

I entered the following poem in a patriotic poem contest held by the nearby Ocala Public
Library. Once again, I did not win, nor did I even receive even so much as a thank you for
entering memo from them.

OUR PATRIOTIC HEARTS
2001

Poems and essays
And stories proclaim
Throughout the world
America's fame.

Anthems and marches,
Choruses galore,
Etchings and paintings,
Parades and much more.

Picnics and speeches
And fireworks on high,
Old Glory flying
So free in the sky.

What causes this fervor
Each impassioned part?
Could it be we're exposing
OUR PATRIOTIC HEARTS?

CHAPTER 5

THE WATERFORD
PERRYSBURG, OHIO

When Pete passed away, my daughters convinced me,
To move back up North, but it was not easy.

I left my nice house in the Florida sun,
And moved to Ohio to *try* to have fun.

My "home" near the Brakels is The Waterford.
I have lots of friends here and never am bored.

We have parties and concerts and do little plays.
Puzzles, and Bingo, and cards fill my days.

The food doesn't suit me, but other than that,
I'm really quite happy in this place that I'm at.

Residents and Staff at The Waterford. I'm the one with the clown nose.

BIRTHDAY WISHES

JAMES UTTER
December 7, 2011

May I *utter* one grand wish for you?
One that I hope will come true,
  May your days all be blessed
  With this thought I possess—
That *every day will be happy not blue.*

JERRY MYERS
December 7, 2011

When I am as old as you,
Perhaps I can bowl as you do.
  That's not likely to be
  For I'm a pessimist, you see.
But, I can send best wishes to you.

MARGE EHMKE
December 20, 2011

Although I don't know you well,
There's a wish I do want to tell.
  May your birthday be merry
  And your days all be very
Enjoyably happy as well.

DORIS MORLOCK
December 25, 2011

Well, I'll be darned!
We've all been charmed
With hula dances along the way,
Now we've learned for sure
Another thing about her—
She was born on Christmas Day!
H A P P Y   B I R T H D A Y
(To both you and your famous partner!)

PAUL BOAT
December 27, 2011

To Paul Boat, a gentleman of note,
I wish a very happy birthday.
You've created many smiles
With your jokes that beguile.

And, oh! By the way, here's one
For you:
What's the longest word in the English
language?
Answer: SMILES—IT STARTS WITH AN "S"
AND ENDS WITH AN "S" with a mile in
between.

SHIRLEY ADAMS
December 2011

(I wrote this for Shirley when she left The
Waterford shortly after I moved in, but I
don't recall the exact date.)

May your time here be thought of with
pleasure,
May you recall special moments to
treasure,
May all of your days glow as brightly
this'n,
May you always remember—
  That it's you ---
    We'll be miss'n'!

FRANCES TESTA
January 13, 2012

To Frances, the most quiet one,
May your days all be filled with great fun;
  May your card games be happy
  And your BINGOS quite snappy
As you play each day away till it's done.

BOB BOND
January 26, 2012

To Bob Bond, woodworker supreme,
May each project become all you can
dream;
      May each corner be square
      And each puzzle quite rare
As you plan each new diabolical scheme.

RUTH ROBERTS
February 5, 2012

To Ruth Roberts, a most quiet lady
Who is shy but never a "fraidy"
      She's a card sharp for sure
      And her actions are pure
And are never shady.

MILLIE LEHR
January 29, 2012

There once was a lady named Millie.
Whose mood could be somber or silly;
      She's a smart one for sure
      And if you knew her,
You'd find that she's really a dilly,
      OR
You'd find she's really a hillbilly?
      OR
You'd find that she's one
f-i-i-i-ne lookin' filly!

PAT SELMEK
January 29, 2012

To Pat Selmek, a lady quite fine,
Each day when we all go to dine;
      She enters with a flair
      As she coaxes that chair
With maneuvers remarkably refined.

GERRY VAN DORN
March 7, 2012

Pretty Gerry Van Dorn
Has no need for a horn
As she enters the dining room with grace.
      She waves and she smiles
      And always beguiles
With a friendly smile on her face.

BARRETT KIFF
March 13, 2012

To Barrett Kiff who is one lucky stiff
To still be walking unassisted,
      Perhaps it's the gal,
      His tail waggin' pal,
Whose antics he's never resisted.

CHARLES FANSLER
April 7, 2012

Charles Fansler, like a gentleman of old,
Is gracious and kind I am told.
      Each birthday it seems
      Appears like a dream,
Demanding best wishes quite bold.

ANN ADAMS
April 9, 2012

To Ann Adams, an outstanding lass.
Whose demeanor is always high class
      Until…she hears something funny,
      Then she's always a honey
And her laughter erupts with a blast.

ROSEMARY STANGE
July 25, 2012

To Rosemary Stange, a player indeed,
Whose game playing skills
Are always in need.

May you always come and play
Since you brighten up our day
And of good players we're always in
need.

BARBARA THIERWECHTER
March 30, 2012

To Barbara Thierwechter, a lady of style,
Whose wardrobe enhances her smile
She's a "star" in my book
When I see her look
Since she always seems to beguile.

TOM GRIMES
March 18, 2012

To watchful Tom Grimes
Whose name rhymes with...rhymes
And is known as a wily instigator.
May he never commit crimes
Or ever spend dimes
To hire his very own Private Litigator!

VIRGINIA PAISIE
April 26, 2012

To Virginia Paisie, a lady of age,
On the 26th you'll turn a page
On that page it will state,
That you definitely rate
A day that will be all the rage
Because...IT'S YOUR BIRTHDAY!

GLORIA KEMP
July 31, 2012

To Gloria Kemp, a "new kid" on the block,
May your first birthday here rock
With best wishes galore
For many, many more,
Like treasures stored in a sock!

LEO THOMAS
July 11, 2012

To Leo Thomas, a farmer of old,
Who now lives where it is cold.
May your days all be sunny
With each a real honey
With a birthday that's spun of pure gold.

HENRY BOND
April 26, 2012

To Henry Bond, a regular fellow,
Whose voice is deep but quite mellow,
On April 26th
It isn't a myth
He'll be one year older so I'll bellow
H A P P Y   B I R T H D A Y!

JACKIE THIERWECHTER
May 10, 2012

Who is as talented as one can be?
Who always smiles sweetly for all to see?
She can take a paintbrush in her little
hand,
Or a fistful of flowers and create
something grand?
Well, I'll be darned! I think I
know!
It's Jackie Thierwechter whose
talents show,
So I'll end this epistle and I will say
HAVE A HAPPY, HAPPY, HAPPY,
HAPPY BIRTHDAY!!!

MILLIE HILL
May 18, 2012

Millie Hill whose talents shine
When she plays cards and that's just fine.
She also sits and chats a while,
And gives to all a friendly smile.

To commemorate in a special way,
I'll wish you well with a
H A P P Y   B I R T H D A Y!

GORDON CONKLIN
May 20, 2012

To Gordon Conklin, a sailor quite fine
Who rode the waves in a dreadful
wartime.
He bravely served his country well,
So to him I'll boldly tell,
H A P P Y   B I R T H D A Y!

EDDIE FELHABER
May 2012

To Eddie Felhaber, a bowler of note,
And a card-playing sharpie
Whose skills get our vote.
The day now has come
That requires me to say,
Have a very, very, very
H A P P Y   B I R T H D A Y

ANN WYMER
May 27, 2012

To dear Ann Wymer
Whose name rhymes with ...rhymer,
There's a wish that is true,
From one rhymer to you.
Have a very, very, very,
H A P P Y   B I R T H D A Y

ANDY DANYKO
May 22, 2012

To Andy Danyko, a prince of a man,
Who helps out his wife
Whenever he can.
Today is a day
When we should all say,
Have a very, very, very,

H A P P Y   B I R T H D A Y!

JOAN WRIGHT
June 5, 2012

To Joan Wright, a retired Air Force lass,
Who always presents a picture of class,
My your day be quite sunny,
And your nose never runny.
Please forgive me if my poetic efforts
seem crass.

JOE CHESTER
June 6, 20 12

To Joe Chester, who has talent galore,
Such as dancing and poker,
And, perhaps even more.
May your birthday be blessed,
Filled with good wishes,
And all of the rest—
But, in case one Happy Birthday was
missed,
Please add my belated wish to the list!
H A P P Y   B I R T H D A Y

NANCY GILMORE
June 6, 2012

To Nancy Gilmore, a lady of action,
Be it books or some other attraction.
I hope your birthday was great
And your greetings not late.

PEG FYE
June 6, 2012

To Peg Fye who flutters by
And offers cheery words here and there,
May your birthday be great
And the good wishes first-rate.

ANDREA MENDIOLA
June 23, 2012

To Andrea, "The Queen of the Nile"
Who honors us with a blink and a smile;
Quite soon we can say to her,
"Hey, it's your day for sure,
So have a great one,
Then proceed as you were."

DOTTY FRANZ
June 23, 2012

To Dotty Franz, a good friend indeed,
Who always runs to help one in need,
May her needs be met
So she will not regret
Having gained one more year with great
speed.

GERI SLAWINSKI
June 26, 2012

To Geri Slawinski, a fine lass indeed.
Who greets everyone warmly with great
speed.
May your birthday be blessed
With lots of Scrabble and the rest,
With you always the winner—that's
decreed!

LAUREN STANGE
July 25, 2012

To Lauren Stange, the elusive one,
Whose smiles tell you that he's having
fun,
        May your birthday be great
        And your greetings not late
As we all celebrate till your birthday is
done.

ROSE ANN STEPHENS
July 10, 2012

To Rose Ann, a lady refined,
Who is always polite and never unkind.
        She always is neat
        From her head to her feet.
Hope your birthday was blessed
With good wishes and the rest.
H A P P Y   B I R T H D A Y

BOB FRENCH
July 26, 2012

To Bob French, a true gentleman,
Who helps a lady with her chair when he
can,
That's more than most men can boast
So *you* deserve a toast.
A n-n-n-d a H-A-P P Y B I R T H D A Y!

WILLIAM DAVIS
July 12, 2012

To William Davis, a most kindly fellow,
Who, at his age, has become even more
mellow.
        May your birthday be blessed
        With good wishes and all of the
rest.
Perhaps your birthday cake will be yellow.

DR. JERRY DEBRUIN
July 10, 2012

Dr. DeBruin, the inquisitive one,
Whose interests embrace everyone.
        May your birthday be sunny
        And your nose never runny,
        (Oops!) May jocularity find you
        And your birthday remind you
That ON THIS DAY YOU SHOULD HAVE
fun!

DR. DZIDRA SHLLAKU
August 18, 2012

To Dzidra Shllaku, a lady of note,
Whose command of many languages
Is a talent remote.
May you always have sunshine
To make each day bright.
May God smile upon you
To make this birthday just right!

DAWN FREISS
August 26, 2012

To Dawn Friess who was born one pretty
August day,
May many birthday wishes be coming
your way.
May there always be sunshine
To make each day bright;
May God smile upon you to make this day
just right!

DON GRIFFITH
August 26, 2012

To affable Don Griffith, a man of renown,
Who often smiles but rarely frowns.
May your birthday be the best—
Even better than all of the rest!

JUDY LEMONS
August 26, 2012

Although I know your birthday has
passed,
I'm sending this to you, late, but at last.
To one who is gentle
With such a friendly smile,
An extremely Happy Birthday
Should always be in style.

MARY YOUNG
August 26, 2012

To Mary Young, a lady of grace,
Whose husband bragged to others
That *she* adorned their place.
May your birthday be merry
With good wishes galore,
And then my wish for you
Is that you will have many, many, more.

MARY ELLEN HARTLEY
August 30, 2012

To Mary Ellen Hartley, a very quiet one,
Who graciously smiles when she's having
fun.
May your birthday be the best
Even better than all of the rest!

SUSAN CAVALEAR
August 31, 2012

To Susan Cavalear who has shown herself
at last,
And I must say—that the facts you
revealed---
Hit us like a blast!
Little did we know that you
Harbored within your room,
A grea-a-t big gorilla
That might predict our doom.
But luckily, Coco is an object,
Rather than a living thing
And we can all rest easily
So that together we can sing,
Happy Birthday to you.

HELEN GRUMMEL
September 18. 2012

(She told me that she loved my poem.
That was high praise, indeed because she
had spent her life teaching English! She
was one grand lady.)

Bet she shorely wuz a purty gal
When she wuz in her teens,
She still ain't too bad lookin'
Considerin' all the years that's gone
between.
And her writin'—o-o-oh it's the bestest
Uv any Ah have evah seen.
Bet she could larn me sumthin'
Iffen Ah wuzn't so dog gone mean.
God bless this purty lady
'cauz the years is flyin' fast
An' WOW! Danged if she ain't havin'
anuther birthday!
Ah shorely do hope she has uh
        BLAST!!!

EMILY SNYDER
September 18, 2012

To Emily Snyder, a fine lass, indeed,
Whose friendly acts of kindness
Comfort those in need.
May this birthday be the best,
Even better than all of the rest.

AUDREY SKINNER
September 3, 2012

To kind Audrey Skinner, a card playing
lass;
When it comes to pinochle,
She has pl-l-l-lenty of class!
And then makes her bid.
There are mighty few among us
Who cannot be "outdid."
So, trundle on, pinochle lady,

Continue your bidding ways.
And then, while you're at it,
Have a wonderfully delightful, belated
        H-A-P-P-Y B-I-R-T-H-D-A-Y

CORBETT RITZMAN
September 18, 2012

To quiet Corbett Ritzman
Who always stands back and observes.
Once in a while you say something
That will throw us for a curve.
As you continue on your way,
Do take time to have a happy birthday.

DOROTHY CHESTER
September 29, 2012

To Dorothy Chester, a bronzed lady
indeed,
Who races through the hallway
At a very spritely speed.
It's all because of the music
That she plays on her radio,
She likes those peppy tunes
That won't allow her to go slow.
So, keep on truckin' kid,
Keep the dial on that music station;
And play it REALLY LOUD
For your birthday celebration!

BILL FRANK
October 7, 2012

To Bill Frank, a fine gentleman, indeed,
Who races through the halls
With great speed.
If I had to guess your age,
I'll admit that I'm not a sage,
So-o-o-o, I'd guess......
For one hundred eight—
You're doing gr-r-r-eat!!!!

MEL AYERS
November 1, 2012

To Mel Ayers, obstetrician supreme,
Hope that your birthday was filled
With all you could dream.
Just imagine all of those babes
You brought into the world—
Those four thousand plus
With their hair all in curls,
What a grand chorus!
How sublime it would be
If they all joined together
To sing HAPPY BIRTHDAY, to thee!!

WAYNE LEATHERMAN
November 11, 2012

To Wayne Leatherman, a fine gentleman
indeed,
Who devoted his life to those who had
needs.
You gave them advice
Which we hope helped them all—
Now *my* advice for your birthday is…

Relax! Celebrate your achievements—
Have a ball!
            H A P P Y   B I R T H D A Y

FRANK SCOTT
April 2013

If I had only known
That your birthday was so near,
I might have written a poem
To wish you lots of cheer.

But I am so darned old, my child,
That for you of tender age,
I'll try to conjure up a wish
That would be worthy of a sage.

I wish for you…the best of…something,
And lots of chicken with your dumplings,
And, if these good things don't come your
way,
I wish for you 99 more Happy Birthdays!

RANDOM ACTS OF KINDNESS

This was an award that was presented to an outstanding employee of The Waterford each
month. The honoree was selected by a committee of residents under the guidance of
Activity Director, Ann Mathews.

NANCY
July 2013

She's jovial and friendly,
And fun to be around,
She performs her tasks in the kitchen
And very rarely frowns.

We especially enjoy the antics
As she mimics our endeavors,
While we are attempting to exercise,
The moves *she* makes are quite clever!

COOKIE
July 2013

They forgot to ask me
To write a little rhyme
So I shrugged my shoulders
And thought...well, that's fine.
But once they nudged
My mind in gear,
Words passed through it
That only I could hear.

So here I go,
I'll have my say
And speak for all

Whom you meet every day.

We like your smile,
Your friendly grace,
Your expertise in administering
To the human race.

You are one of those people
Who is always there
Doing whatever is needed
With loving care.

SHARITA LEWIS
July 2013

Sharita, Sharita, where've
You been so long?
        Sharita, Sharita,.....hmmmm.
Kinda sounds like a cowboy song.
But, as I sit and try out rhymes,
I think of all the many times
When I have seen Sharita.

We all have seen her race through the
halls
Rushing to make her morning calls.

Then we might see her leading a class,
My goodness! She's a versatile lass.

But no matter where this lady is,
She'll induce a laugh, or at least a grin
To make us feel better
In the place we're in.
When we have seen Sharita.

Many thanks for a job well done
And making it seem like such great fun.

MARY
July 2013

For it was M-a-r-y, M-a-r-y,
Plain as any name could be,
So the song goes, but today
Our Mary is the one we see.

She's a lady of the evening---
Since she works mostly at night.
She concocts the hallway bulletin boards
Making sure the info is right.

She distributes special notices
But doesn't miss any calls;
She carries her phone along
And takes care of one and all.

Why, she's a regular "Johnny on the
Spot"
But, how can that be?
You thought I said her name was Mary?

Yep! She's the one we see.

Thanks so much for the job you do.

Your many fine talents are shining through.

FRANK SCOTT, THE DRIVER
August 29, 2013

What can one say about Frank?
Our driver who reigns supreme;
    A trip to the store
    May seem like a chore
But could turn out to be
More than it seems.

He loads and unloads,
Knows all the roads,
And the winners of yesterday's games.
He sometimes invokes a laugh or a joke,
After which we'll never be the same.

The thought that I'll savor
That has a tickle-bone flavor
Is the tattoo he wants to get—
    On his knee!
As ridiculous as it may seem
He'll realize his fondest dream---
And there forever after there will be
His very own BANJO on his knee

A thousand thanks to Frank!

ZZZZZZZZZZZZZZZZZZZZZZZZZZZZZZZZZ

JEFF AND DIANE WAGNER
November 15, 2013

To generous Jeff Wagner
Who volunteers his time
Conducting the Bingo sessions
That instigated this rhyme.

So joyous are we residents
When we can make a BINGO call!
And know that we are envied
By the players one and all.

Please know that we are thankful
For your deftly administered deeds.

The world would be a better place
If all others followed your lead.

We also must honor your wife,
Whose snacks set us aglow,
With sincere appreciation
For the exemplary talents *she* shows.

Many thanks to both of you
for your thoughtful
service to others.

PASTOR CURTIS MILLER
November 23, 2013

To Pastor Curtis,
Bible scholar supreme,
He can quote more verses

Than we could ever dream.
He preaches and he teaches,
Yet he enjoys a good joke.

He's not highfalutin'
He's just plain old 'good folks.'

His cooking is legend,
His generosity, grand.

We kinda like him lo-o-ots
With one of his treats in our hand!
Thank *you* for sharing *all*
Of your many talents so unselfishly!

SUSIE WAIBLE-ROSE
February 2014

To Susie Waible-Rose,
A true Christian indeed
Who organizes church services
That serve Catholic needs.

She procures and schedules
Each facet of this endeavor,
And we must finally conclude
That she is very clever!

MY GOSH, IT'S JOSH
February 2014

Who is the waiter that smiles the most?
Who greets each person like a gracious
host?
Who is the one who is as polite as can be
Whenever he waits on you or on me?

Who serves each diner as if it's a pleasure

And tries hard to give that extra
measure?
You may have guessed it,
This is not a lot of bosh—
And you know it is true…because…
MY GOSH! IT'S JOSH!

JONATHAN STOUT
September 2014

To Jonathon Stout, college student
supreme,
Who epitomizes many coed's dreams,
He's tall, dark, and handsome
But he's more than he seems.

Did you go to the luau dance?
Oh! My! Gracious me!
Were you there?
Did you see?

Jonathon donned a grass skirt
And did that hula thing.
Heavens to Betsy!
You should have seen him swing!

And, then, he did the Chicken dance
Where he sang and strutted and literally
pranced!
In a nut shell, John is a gem.
If you want something done, just ask him.

DEBBIE FARBROTHER
November 2014

Debbie Farbrother is the best.
She loves her job, and never seems to rest.
She speaks to all with a courteous, friendly, greeting.
Which makes that person feel happy for the meeting.

If anyone asks her status,
Don't hesitate…be BOLD!
Step forward and speak LOUDLY,
"In case you haven't been told,
Debbie is among the very top
Of the entire Waterford crop.

TERESA AND STEVE
March 15, 2015

To Teresa and Steve who are the best!
May your generous nature be blest.
We do love your Saturday games
Which have earned for you much name.

When Bingo! Bingo! rings out,
It's because of you that we shout.

For a wee bit of candy from you,
We're way over zealous, it's true.

But we really DO LOVE YOU, TOO!
And to prove it, here are our many thankful names.
(We all signed our names around the edges of the poem.)

TOM ROHWEDER
May 22, 2015

To Tom who is a juggler,
A whistler, and a nurse.
He handles his talents well
Which are an asset—not a curse.

We all applaud his efforts,
His congeniality and skill.

He exhibits a friendly smile
As he distributes those pills.

He must be totally exhausted
At the end of each day
Because he walk miles
As he passes our way.

LESLIE TATRO
May 22, 2015

To Leslie Tatro who is efficient,
Dedicated, and true,
To her lofty ambitions
Which can be attained by only a few.

May your goal that requires
Patience, diligence, and knowledge
Pay off in the end
When you have finished college.

Then we can brag about and claim,
"Why, we knew Doctor Tatro
 When she was just a kid,

But, my goodness! She's a doctor!
Just look at what she did!

****

My grandson, Wayne Brakel, was about to leave for a three week trip to Hofu, Japan where he would spend about ten days each with two different families. He was to travel with a group of students in a student exchange program from Monroe, Michigan.

Wayne had rarely stayed away overnight so I thought he might need a little encouragement while he was gone.

THIS, TOO, SHALL PASS
July 14 2012

When you are beset with dreadful fears,
Remember this, my dearest of dears,
Just let these words run through your head,
Remembering they are words your Grammy said,
"THIS, TOO, SHALL PASS and I'll survive,
Why, I'm one smart kid and, heck,
I'LL STILL BE ALIVE!"

THE SPAGHETTI SAUCE SAGA
November 29, 2012

She's one of the best dressed
That we've ever seen,
She presents herself well,
'Cause heck! She's our queen!

But, once in a while
She lets her hair down,
She does uncommon things
But becomes more renowned.

When the fire alarm rang—
My goodness! Did...it...**ring!**
Cheryl rushed toward the fire
Doing her "I'm in charge thing!"

It seems that she, alone,

Put out the blaze
And rescued the woman who'd created
This spaghetti sauce haze.

But while she was performing
This very heroic act,
The sprinklers kicked in—
She got soaked! That's a fact!

The alarm kept on beeping
And as she raced down the halls
Peg Fye tossed her a towel
Which she caught like a ball.

"A cooking fire on the third floor
Has now been put out.

153

Go back in your rooms!"
Was her warning shout.

When the hubbub was over,
Four fire trucks drove away.
The policemen probably found some donuts
To wind up their day.

We residents, too,
Had had enough for one day,
So we all donned our night clothes
Then one by one hit the hay.
But we shook our heads in wonder,

In fact, absolute awe---
Was that bedraggled-looking wet thing
really Cheryl?
Who streaked through the halls!

But Cheryl Hartman???
Well.....it's now eight weeks later
And she can still be seen
Supervising the clean-up
'Cause heck! She's our queen.

WE THANK YOU
FOR STANDING TALL
Your appreciative residents

****

My daughter, Lisa Brakel, is a school librarian. In addition to her regular duties, she also sponsored a book club for students who arranged an annual poetry slam. She asked me to write a poem to kick off the event in 2013. Here it is:

POETRY SLAM
April 23, 2013

Good evening my poetic friends,
May all of your voices in rhythm blend
May all of your poems contain good rhymes
And your electronic toys be left behind.

Turn off your cell phones-
Do it at once!
If any are heard,
You'll be a dunce.

With that having been said,
I'll step out of the way.
Let us hear *your* poems,
As *you* have your say.

So-o-o
Abrakadabra!
Ali kazam!
Let's us get on with our
Very first POETRY SLAM!

****

The following poem was written for Hilda Schmidt, who had appeared in one of our resident skits for a talent show. She played the part of a lady who had huge breasts, which were really inflated balloons. A man was asking her to be his Valentine. She rejected him.

After the skit, the balloons were delivered to my room. I left them in my pantry for a long time. During that period I had asked Hilda to repair a pair of jeans for me, which she did. I had recently learned that she l-o-o-o-ved tomatoes so much that she would have some every day of the year that they were available.

This poem was actually meant as a thank you but wound up in a tomato box on her chair at dinner one night. I placed the two balloons side by side inside the box.

Hilda looked at the box on her chair, saw the balloons and said, "Looks like boobs to me!" Well, now, Hilda was usually a person who enjoyed a good joke but I was never sure whether she thought my "joke" was funny or not.

HILDA, MY HILDA
November 11, 2013

Hilda, my Hilda,
It's just about time,
That your name was emblazoned
In an asinine rhyme.

Your good deeds are legend,
Your fetishes, many,
And considering your ideas,
You rarely lack any.

However, I remember
As our hearts swelled with pride
When you had these "knockers"
Long after you were a bride.

Now they are diminished –
Deflation has set in
I doubt that you will ever want
To use them again.

Perhaps the enclosed will appease you
Since growing old makes us sad;
But you still have these,
So you ain't doin' too bad!

(Written with love and many, many thanks for replacing the elastic in my jeans.)

THE UGLIEST GIFT
Christmas—Lady's Tea White Elephant Gift Exchange 2013

I know this is the ugliest gift
That you have ever craved,
But when my dear sweet Pete (my husband) died,
I found a tool like this and raved!

There is a God in Heaven,
Of that I am quite sure.
Since I was now the master
Of those pliers that made me purr.

I don't have to beg male relatives
Or waiters, workmen or worse,
I can now open almost any bottle
"Cause I carry *this tool* in my purse!

(Pat Selmek, another resident of the Independent Living unit of The Waterford where I lived was not thrilled with the gift. I thought it would be funny. I guess I have a weird sense of humor.)

The following poem was written at the request of Dotty Franz. I had given her a little replica of a bathroom stool. It was really a white pencil eraser. She wanted it for the birthdays of two young, male relatives. The poem was to be a riddle—the boys had to guess what it could be used for.

THE BIRTHDAY THINGAMAJIG
2014

Don't expect this little gadget
To take care of bathroom things
'Cause if you drop a coin in inside
You won't even hear it PING!

But, if you are adding 2 plus 2
And for the answer you write 45,
Get rid of it QUICK and change it

Or your teacher may skin you alive!!!!!

P.S. If you use this thingamajig properly,
Then, do not fear, my dears,
You WILL stay alive.

WHAT IS A THINGAMAJIG?

****

Written for Dotty Franz after she fell down 15 concrete steps at a church event. The whole left side of her face was bruised.

TOPSY- TURVY LADIES
May 1, 2014

When topsy-turvy ladies
Go a tumblin' down the trail
'Cause they have missed the shiny thang
'At's used fer guidance rails.

Be thankful that yer undies
Wuz kivered with yer slacks
And that all uv yore appendages
Follerd in yer tracks.

'Twas said that all yer pieces

Are still attached to you;
Cain't y'all see, my chile,
There ain't no reason ta be blue.

But black an blue 'tis what you are—
Gee, an', I always thought you wuz a
white girl,
H-m-m-m......

P.S. If this little epistle doesn't make you
feel better, nothing will.

****

TRIBUTE TO LISA AT 55
December 2014

May your day be one to remember.
May your year be one to enjoy.

May your home always be happy,

156

And filled with your three wonderful
boys.

And then, think of your "dear" mother,
The one who has loved you the most.
Why, I knew you before you were born!
Of that, I'm the only one who can boast.

Why, I changed your old dirty diaper
And wiped up your little snotty nose,
Then, suddenly you were a lady!
And, now... I rest in repose.

The tables have turned unbearably
Since *you* are taking care of *me*—
You have brushed my old crumby
dentures
Thus each day becomes an *adventure!*

So! No matter where you go,
No matter what you do,
Remember—I have loved you the
longest!
　　　　(55 years and 9 months)
So toil away, give me only what is due.

****

WHO IS BEN CRANE'S GRANDMOTHER?
October 8, 2015

When I first moved to The Waterford (a retirement home) one of the first people I met was a lady named Ann Adams. When I went to the dining room for breakfast, she and I always sat at the same table that seated 6-8 people. There was Ann and I, Tom Grimes, Bill Frank, Andrea Mendiola, Norma Nelson, and Paul Boat. It was Tom Grimes who dubbed the group, "The Breakfast Club." In the evening we were joined by a lady named Jo Van Dyne.

My daughter, Lisa Brakel, lived at Temperance, Michigan. Lisa had an acquaintance there named Leslie Crane whose son, Ben Crane, attended Bedford High School with Lisa's son, Wayne. Eventually Lisa learned through the grapevine that Ben Crane's grandmother also lived at The Waterford. She asked me if I knew Ben Crane's grandmother and I didn't believe that I did, but I began listening carefully for someone to mention their grandson, Ben. Time passed and Lisa would periodically ask again if I had found Ben Crane's grandmother.

A year or two later, in desperation, I asked one day at breakfast, "Does anyone here know of anyone who lives here and has a grandson named Ben Crane?" Ann looked over at me and said, "That would be ME!" What a shock!

I had tried to find someone for about two years and, there she was, sitting across the same table as I had all of these months. What a surprise!

But, wait---there is more to the story. Read on.

WHO WAS ANN ADAM'S SECRET FRIEND?
October 8, 2015

One year in February Ann Mathews, the activity director at The Waterford, suggested that we draw the name of someone in our group who would be our "secret friend." The name I drew was Ann Adams. We were to "secretly" plant a "clue" along with a suggestive gift for our "friend" for three days in a row, then on the fourth day we gave our last clue and named who we thought was our "secret friend."

Following are the clues I gave:

> From whence we came
> To where we be,
> We share the same,
> Both you and me.

The answer was that we both moved from our homes and we both had apartments at the Waterford. (The gift I gave her was a recipe for "Rum Cake.")

This was my second clue:

> Where flowers bloom
> And robins sing
> I'll go there now
> To do my thing.

The answer was the courtyard. At that time it was my habit to go outside after dinner for a while before going back to my apartment. The courtyard was just outside of the dining room.

My third clue was this:

> If you could just remember
> The things that we both share
> You'd know me for the place I go
> For the doing of the hair.

At that time both she and I had our weekly shampoo and set at the third floor beauty salon. The gift I gave her was a playing card holder. Many card games were played in the Activity Room but I found out later that she didn't even play cards.

Fourth Clue:

MAY I HAVE SOME PEPPER, PLEASE?
AND DO PASS ME THE SALT.
I HOPE YOU'LL KNOW ME BY MY NAME
FOR THESE HINTS HAVE COME TO A HALT.
MY NAME IS __ __ __ __ __.

She did not guess who I was.

But....the story is not finished. After we had given the first hint, when I gave her the recipe for rum cake, Ann very cleverly passed the recipe on to *her* secret friend, Jo van Dyne, who sat beside me across the table from Ann!

The very last gift that I gave Ann was a little bucket with holes.

FILL YOUR BUCKET WITH D-R-E-A-M-S !!!
Never mind the holes----
You can plug them up with
B-U-B-B-L-E-----G U M.
YOUR SECRET FRIEND,
LEONA M. SMITH

****

THE WAY KIDS SAY IT,
(Or, THE WAY KIDS SPELL IT OUT)

I taught first, second, or third graders for 34 years. Here are a few of the gems that I recorded for future use –like today—October 27, 2015. I loved to read their spelling sentences and other writings.

Write the meaning of each of the following words:

lad—"a place where people work"

clan—"like a clam in a shell"

lint—"like you put in your lighter"

slot—"like you tore a hole in your clothes"
   --- "like a cement slot"

flat—"like a pink cake"

stall—"like a stall of corn"

mill—"like someone cooks a mill"

pill—"like you pill your milk"

feast—"like an animal"

lease—"it goes around a dog's neck"

beam—"a big flame"

rear—"like someone has a rear in their pants"

pleat—"like someone says ,'Pleat give me a pencil.'"

defeat—"like you trip over your feet"

wax—"like you get 7 wax for your birthday"

pot pie—"like the Pot Pie and Janie show"

hatching—"like you are hatching a tree"

****

During the winter months when we had a Snow Day, the students stayed home and had to do "snow packs," which were made up of work sheet assignments. One homework assignment that I gave was: List one thing that you did while you were at home:

"I sighed all my valentines."

I said: Write the name of a story that you really like.

"Winnie the Poor."

I said: Write a sentence using the word "forever."

"Can I ask a forever?" (Did he mean favor?)

I said: Write a sentence using the word "nighttime."

"At nighttime the ghosts sprowl."

Creative writing—Tell about a personal experience that you have had.

160

"I burned myself so bad that I had to go to the emergency award. I still have the scare."

Write a sentence telling how two things are alike:

"Measles and mumps are alike because both are fowl."

Use a descriptive word to tell about these foods (which were pictured):

booled vegetables	scranbled eggs
caned vegetables	boilded eggs

Question: How often should you eat vegetables?

"At least two or three times."

Question: Name one thing you can do to prevent cavities.

"Cut down on sweet smacks."

Teacher: Who else lives at your house besides you mother?

"My dad—he's not my real dad, but he's better than nothing."

****

Edna Rideout was a lifetime resident of Toledo, Ohio. At the time of this writing, she was also a resident of The Waterford, a retirement home in Perrysburg, Ohio. That is where we met. She related the following stories to me (used here with her permission). Edna and her husband were vacationing in Florida where this conversation took place. A lady that she had met in Florida was asking her these questions.

TWO-LEE-DEW
November 4, 2015

She studied the map and muttered,
"Two-lee-dew? Two-lee-dew?
Where *is* this place called Two-lee-dew?"

I shook my head because I never knew
Nor had I ever *heard*
Of a place called Two-lee-dew.

I asked, "Is this place *here*,
In *this* country?"
"Well, I guess it surely must be."

I asked, "Can you give us just one small clue?
About this place called Two-lee-dew?
I was told that it was in O-hi-o,

Now do you know?

Now, do you know?"

I glanced at her map,
And in a flash! I knew! I *knew*!
About this place called Two-lee-dew!

I laughed and laughed
Till my face turned red.

I turned to her and laughingly said,

"Why, I lived right there in Two-lee-dew,
But I never knew, I *never knew*
That anyone said it the way that you do.

Everyone there who is in '*the know*'
Pronounces it like Toe-lee-dough.
To-le-do!"

AUNT MARGARETE
November 4, 2015

Edna Rideout and some of her relatives were enjoying a party in a downstairs living room. Someone asked, "Where is Aunt Margarete?" Now, Aunt Margarete was a self-claimed expert on most things. No one ever agreed with her opinions, nor did anyone ever want to hear her opinions.

In response to the query about where she was, someone at the party answered, "She's upstairs."

Another person asked, "Why isn't she here at the party? This is her own house."

Another person triumphantly replied, "*She* wasn't invited!"

****

MY MERRY OLD ROCKING CHAIR
2015

I'm just an old retired teacher,
My students have gone their own way
So I'm thinking of many possibilities,
Now that I have time to play.

I yearned to become a dancer
Where I would become a famous Rockette.
But, then I also wanted to sing opera
And appear on the stage at the Met.

So, now, I'm thinking I'll compose a concerto
Which people will beg me to perform,
Then...I look at my crooked old fingers...
They aren't the same ones with which I was born.

Oh, well...I always wanted to run in a marathon;
However, my attempts would be a disgrace,
Why, if I pushed my old walker to the limit,
People would laugh right out loud at my pace.

Yes, all of those unfilled dreams haunt me;
They race around and around in my head,
So my merry old rocking chair is my haven
Where I'd rather live on dreams than be *dead!!!*

Leona Smith

POSTSCRIPT

There once was a lady named Leona
Whose poems were full of balogna
The neighbors said, "They stink
And we're on the brink
Of drowning her in rancid cologna."

****

Editor's Note: Leona M. Smith spent most of 2015 compiling her poetry into this book. She thoroughly enjoyed revisiting the memories these poems sparked. My sister sent me her manuscript and I began editing it in November 2015. Sadly, as she and I neared the end of the project, she contracted pneumonia and died on December 26, 2015. This was the obituary I wrote for her:

On behalf of the family we're sorry to say,
Leona May (Heramb) Smith has passed away.
Late of The Waterford, Perrysburg, Ohio,
Her loved ones were near her when she did die-o.

Born as a Heramb she had siblings-a dozen!
Most have now passed but they spawned many cousins.
Jennilee (Heramb) Smith does still survive,
The last of the thirteen kids still left alive.

The day after Christmas in 1953,
Leona wed Wayne Allen Smith with great glee.
The day after Christmas in 2015,
Was the last day on Earth that Leona was seen.

Leona's dear husband died in 2010,
She's now reunited with Wayne Smith again.
Lisa E. Brakel and Lori L. Smith,
Her daughters will mourn her, along with their kith.

Lori is a spinster but Lisa is not,
Timothy D. Brakel's the husband she's got.
They have two kids, Brammer C. and Wayne P.
They'll miss their Grammy a lot more than thee.

A Bachelor's and Master's from old ISU,
Led Leona to teaching and years quickly flew.

Maryland School first, then Durgan, but wait,
Oxford Elementary is where she got great.

In addition to teaching, she was a fine poet.
(We've done this in rhyme so all now will know it.)
She wrote poems for staff events, poems for kids.
She wrote them to thank people for what they did.

She was an inventor, or so some would say.
She made a nice cabinet--The Display-Away.
It held all you'd need to make bulletin boards.
Fleetwood Furniture built it and sold it to the hordes.

Another design which had many a fan,
Was known as "Leona's Lifetime Lesson Plan."
Yes, she was creative and none can dispute it.
(She did not write this poem, so this can't refute it.)

In mid-1990 she retired with her spouse,
And enjoyed many years in a Florida house.
When Wayne passed away, she thought it was best,
To return to her roots, back in the Midwest.

She moved to a "home" near the Brakels and found,
New friends and fun things to do all around.
She played bingo and cards and bought lottery tickets,
Did jigsaw puzzles for hours till the last piece she'd click it.

She spent 2015 working diligently,
Compiling her poems into a book you could see.
The daughters will make sure that project gets done,
And then let folks know where to get themselves one.

She's now been cremated and will rest all her days
With her husband in Florida's warm golden rays.
And so as we end we'll give her the last word,
We think she'd be happy to know that you've heard:

"May the joys of this season embrace you,
May gratitude charmingly grace you,
May the warmness of friendships caress you,
May God in his firmament bless you."

INDEX

166

Made in the USA
Charleston, SC
29 February 2016